Experiencing the Depths of Jesus Christ

Library of Spiritual Classics

This is Volume Two of a unique library of great Christian literature. It is a collection covering only one theme: how to experience Christ, in the depths.

Volume One is entitled *Practicing His Presence* and is a compilation of writings on that subject by Frank Laubach and Brother Lawrence. We feel that it is one of the finest introductions on getting to know the Lord more intimately that has ever been published.

As to the present volume, Jeanne Guyon left two great contributions to Christendom and to church history: her autobiography and this little book. It is almost impossible to calculate the great position this book holds in the history of the church. It is probably the most famous and influential Christian book ever written by a woman. Will Durant, in his eleven-volume history of mankind, *The Story of Civilization*, devotes several pages to the life of Madame Guyon and her writings, centering primarily on her autobiography and three of her books. The most influential of these is the book *Le Moyen Court et Très Facile de Faire Oraison*, now published in English under the title of *Experiencing the Depths of Jesus Christ*. The woman Madame Guyon and this little book had a great impact on the entire nation of France, shaking even the throne of Louis XIV. Through the ages, it has continued to influence the lives of many, including some of the most respected names in church history.

Experiencing the Depths of Jesus Christ

JEANNE GUYON

Formerly Entitled:

SHORT AND VERY EASY

METHOD OF PRAYER;

WHICH ALL CAN PRACTICE WITH THE GREATEST FACILITY, AND ARRIVE IN A SHORT TIME, BY ITS MEANS, AT A HIGH DEGREE OF PERFECTION.

BY MADAME GUYON.

CHRISTIAN BOOKS
AUGUSTA, MAINE

Second printing, May 1980
Third printing, June 1981

ISBN 0-940232-00-6

Printed in the United States of America

Christian Books Publishing House
Box 959
Augusta, Maine
207-582-4880

ACKNOWLEDGEMENT

To read the original of this book was like finding a very ancient, faded painting that had been put aside because its features had long ago become indistinct under endless layers of varnish. The beholder could see that perhaps some beautiful work of art might lie beneath the surface, but restoring it to its original beauty would be a formidable task indeed.

So it was with Jeanne Guyon's "little book." Little by little, layer after layer, the varnish had to be stripped away until finally there emerged a rare, exquisite masterpiece.

It was Linda and Vicki, two very dear young ladies from Tennessee, who set out to painstakingly remove those countless layers which obscured the depth and simplicity of this book. For the first time the thoughts of Jeanne Guyon have come to life in clear, modern language.

All of us who read and enjoy these pages will be forever grateful to you both.

CONTENTS

Preface

Written in the latter part of the
Seventeenth Century

This little book, conceived in great simplicity, was not written to be published. I wrote it for a few individuals who desired to love God with all their hearts. But because of the profit they received from reading the manuscript, many asked to obtain their own personal copy. It was because of these requests that this little book was commited to the press.

I have left the book in its original simplicity. It contains no criticism of the teachings of others who have written concerning spiritual things. On the contrary, it enforces those teachings.

I now submit the entire book to the judgment of learned and experienced men with but this request: Please do not stop at the surface but enter into my main purpose in writing. That purpose is to induce the whole world to love God and to serve Him in a way that is easier and simpler than any could imagine.

I have intentionally written this book to those dear, simple followers of Jesus Christ who are not qualified for intensive research but who, nonetheless, desire to be wholly given to God.

The reader who comes to this book—without prejudice—will find, hidden beneath the simplest expressions, a secret unction. This unction will excite him to seek after that inward happiness which all the Lord's disciples should wish to lay hold of and enjoy.

I have stated that *perfection* can easily be attained, and this is true. Jesus Christ is *perfection,* and when we seek Him within ourselves, He is easily found.

But perhaps you will reply, "Did the Lord not sav. 'You shall seek me and shall not find me.'?" (John 7:34) Ah, but your Lord, who cannot contradict Himself, also said to all, "Seek, and you *shall* find." (Matthew 7:7)

Yes, it is true, if you seek the Lord and yet are unwilling to stop your sinning, you shall not find Him. Why? Because you are seeking Him in a place where He is not. Therefore, it is said, "You shall die in your sins."

But if you will take the trouble to seek God in your own heart, and if you sincerely forsake your sins so that you may draw near to Him, you shall infallibly find Him.

I realize that the prospect of living a "life of piety" is frightening to most Christians! And prayer is viewed as a very difficult attainment. Consequently, most believers are too discouraged at the very outset even to take the first step in this direction. It is true that if you consider the difficulty of some new undertaking it can surely cause you to despair and make you reluctant to begin. On the other hand, the desirableness of such an adventure—and the idea that it may easily be accomplished—can cause you to launch out with vigor.

This book, therefore, lights the way to the desirability, the pleasure, the advantages and the ease of these two matters: *prayer* and *piety*.

Oh, if only once we could be convinced of God's

goodness towards His children and of His desire to reveal Himself to them! We would no longer seek our own selfish desires. We would not be so quickly discouraged from pursuing what He is so longing to give us.

> He who spared not His own Son, but delivered Him up for us all, how shall He not, with Him, also freely give us all things?
>
> (Romans 8:32)

We only need a little courage and perseverance. Actually, we have enough of both in our earthly affairs, but none at all in the only thing that really matters. (Luke 10:42)

Some of you may doubt that God can actually be found so easily. If so, do not merely take my word for it. Instead, try for yourselves what I am proposing to you. For I am sure that your own experience will convince you that the reality is far greater than what I have told you.

Beloved reader, read this little book with a sincere and honest spirit. Read it in lowliness of mind without the inclination to criticize. If you do, you will not fail to reap profit from it. *I have written this book with a desire that you might wholly give yourself to God.*

Please receive this book with that same desire in your own heart.

This book has no other purpose than this: to invite the simple and the child-like to approach their Father...a Father who delights in seeing the humble confidence of His children and is grieved by their distrust.

Therefore, with a sincere desire for your own salvation, seek nothing from this book except *the love of God.* With such an expectation you shall assuredly obtain that love.

I am not saying that this way is better than that of someone else. I am only honestly declaring, from my own experience and that of others, the joy found in following the Lord in this way.

There are many other subjects we could touch upon—things of great spiritual significance—but because they do not immediately relate to our main subject, experiencing Jesus Christ, they have been omitted. Without a doubt, nothing will be found here that will offend if only the little book is read in the same spirit in which it was written. Even more certainly, those who earnestly make trial of this way will find that I have written the truth.

> Oh Holy Jesus, it is You alone who love the simple and innocent. It is Your "delight to dwell with the children of men," (Proverbs 8:3) with those who are willing to become "little children." (Matthew 18:3) You are the only One who can cause this little book to be of any value. Beloved Lord, write it on the hearts of those who read it and lead them to seek You within themselves. It is there that You rest, as in the manger, waiting to receive proofs of their love and to give them testimonies of Yours in return. Oh, it is true that the fault is theirs for not experiencing all that You are so willing to give. And yet—oh, Child Almighty, Uncreated Love, Silent and All-containing

Word—it is really up to You to make Yourself loved, enjoyed and understood. You can do it, and I know that You will do it in this little book, for it belongs entirely to You; it came wholly out of You; and it points only to You.

Jeanne Guyon
Grenoble, France
about 1685

Experiencing the Depths of Jesus Christ

1

From the Shallows To the Depths

As you pick up this book, you may feel that you simply are not one of those people capable of a deep experience with Jesus Christ. Most Christians do not feel that *they* have been called to a deep, inward relationship to their Lord. But we have all been called to the depths of Christ just as surely as we have been called to salvation.

When I speak of this "deep, inward relationship to Jesus Christ," what do I mean? Actually, it is very simple. It is only the turning and yielding of your heart to the Lord. It is the expression of love within your heart for Him.

You will recall that Paul encourages us to "pray without ceasing." (I Thessalonians 5:17) The Lord also invites us to "watch and pray." (Mark 13:33,37) It is apparent from these two verses, as well as many more, that we all live by this kind of experience, this *prayer*, just as we live by love.

Once the Lord spoke and said, "I counsel you to buy from me gold tried in the fire that you may be rich." (Revelation 3:18) Dear reader, there is gold available to you. This gold is much more easily obtained than you could ever imagine. It is available to *you*. The purpose of this book is to launch you into this exploration and into this discovery.

I give you an invitation: If you are thirsty, come to the living waters. Do not waste your precious time digging wells that have no water in them. (John 7:37; Jeremiah 2:13)

If you are starving and can find nothing to satisfy your hunger, then come. Come, and you will be filled.

You who are poor, come.

You who are afflicted, come.

You who are weighted down with your load of wretchedness and your load of pain, come. You *will* be comforted!

You who are sick and need a physician, come. Don't hesitate because you have diseases. Come to your Lord and show Him all your diseases, and they will be healed!

Come!

Dear child of God, your Father has His arms of love open wide to you. Throw yourself into His arms. You who have strayed and wandered away as sheep, return to your Shepherd. You who are sinners, come to your Savior.

I especially address those of you who are very simple and you who are uneducated, even you who cannot read and write. You may think you are the one person *most* incapable of this abiding experience of Christ, this prayer of simplicity. You may think yourself the one farthest from a deep experience with the Lord; but, in fact, the Lord has *especially* chosen you! You are the one *most* suited to know Him well.

So let no one feel left out. Jesus Christ has called us all.

Oh, I suppose there is one group who *is* left out!

Do not come if you have no heart. You see, before you come, there is one thing you must do: You must first give your heart to the Lord.

"But I do not know how to give my heart to the Lord."

Well, in this little book you will learn what it means to give your heart to the Lord and how to make that gift to Him.

Let me ask you, then, do you desire to know the Lord in a deep way? God *has* made such an experience, such a walk, possible for you. He has made it possible through the grace He has given to *all* His redeemed children. He has done it by means of His Holy Spirit.

How then will you come to the Lord to know Him in such a deep way? Prayer is the key. But I have in mind a certain kind of prayer. It is a kind of prayer that is very simple and yet holds the key to perfection and goodness—things found only in God Himself. The type of prayer that I have in mind will deliver you from enslavement to every sin. It is a prayer that will release to you every Godly virtue.

You see, the only way to be perfect is to walk in the presence of God. The only way you can live in His presence in uninterrupted fellowship is by means of prayer, but a very special kind of prayer. It is a prayer that leads you into the presence of God and keeps you there at all times; a prayer that can be experienced under any conditions, any place, and any time.

Is there really such a prayer? Does such an experience

with Christ truly exist?

Yes, there is such a prayer! A prayer that does not interfere with your outward activities or your daily routine.

There is a kind of prayer that can be practiced by kings, by priests, by soldiers, by laborers, by children, by women, and even by the sick.

May I hasten to say that the kind of prayer I am speaking of is not a prayer that comes from your mind. It is a prayer that begins in the heart. It does not come from your understanding or your thoughts. Prayer offered to the Lord from your mind simply would not be adequate. Why? Because your mind is very limited. The mind can pay attention to only one thing at a time. Prayer that comes out of the heart is not interrupted by thinking! I will go so far as to say that nothing can interrupt this prayer, *the prayer of simplicity*.

Oh yes, there is *one* thing. Selfish desires can cause this prayer to cease. But even here there is encouragement, for once you have enjoyed your Lord and tasted the sweetness of His love, you will find that even your selfish desires no longer hold any power. You will find it impossible to have pleasure in anything except Him.

I realize that some of you may feel that you are very slow, that you have a poor understanding, and that you are very unspiritual. Dear reader, there is nothing in this universe that is easier to obtain than the enjoyment of Jesus Christ! Your Lord is more present to you than you are to yourself! Furthermore, His desire to give Himself to you is *greater* than *your* desire to lay hold of Him.

How, then, do you begin? You need only one thing. You need only to know how to seek Him. When you have found the way to seek Him, you will discover that this way to God is more natural and easier than taking a breath.

By this "prayer of simplicity," this *experiencing* of Christ deep within, you may live by God Himself with less difficulty and with less interruption than you now live by the air which you take into you. If this is true, then I ask, wouldn't it be a sin not to pray? Yes, it would be a sin. But once you have learned how to seek Jesus Christ and how to lay hold of Him, you will find the way so easy that you will no longer neglect this relationship to your Lord.

Let us go on, therefore, and learn this simple way to pray.

2

Launching Out

I would like to address you as though you were a beginner in Christ, one seeking to know Him. In so doing, let me suggest two ways for you to come to the Lord. I will call the first way "praying the Scripture;" the second way I will call "beholding the Lord" or "waiting in His presence."

"Praying the Scripture" is a unique way of dealing with the Scripture; it involves both reading and prayer.

Here is how you should begin.

Turn to the Scripture; choose some passage that is simple and fairly practical. Next, come to the Lord. Come quietly and humbly. There, before Him, read a small portion of the passage of Scripture you have opened to.

Be careful as you read. Take in fully, gently and carefully what you are reading. Taste it and digest it as you read.

In the past it may have been your habit, while reading, to move very quickly from one verse of Scripture to another until you had read the whole passage. Perhaps you were seeking to find the main point of the passage.

But in coming to the Lord by means of "praying the

Scripture," you do not read quickly; you read very slowly. You do not move from one passage to another, not until you have *sensed* the very heart of what you have read.

You may then want to take that portion of Scripture that has touched you and turn it into prayer.

After you have sensed something of the passage and after you know that the essence of that portion has been extracted and all the deeper sense of it is gone, then, very slowly, gently, and in a calm manner begin to read the next portion of the passage. You will be surprised to find that when your time with the Lord has ended, you will have read very little, probably no more than half a page.

"Praying the Scripture" is not judged by *how much* you read but by the *way* in which you read.

If you read quickly, it will benefit you little. You will be like a bee that merely skims the surface of a flower. Instead, in this new way of reading with prayer, you must become as the bee who penetrates into the *depths* of the flower. You plunge deeply within to remove its deepest nectar.

Of course, there is a kind of reading the Scripture for scholarship and for study—but not here. That studious kind of reading will not help you when it comes to matters that are *divine!* To receive any deep, inward profit from the Scripture, you must read as I have described. Plunge into the very depths of the words you read until revelation, like a sweet aroma, breaks out upon you.

I am quite sure that if you will follow this course, little by little you will come to experience a very rich prayer that flows from your inward being.

Let us move now to the second kind of prayer, which I mentioned earlier.

The second kind of prayer, which I described as "beholding the Lord" or "waiting on the Lord," *also* makes use of the Scripture but it is not actually a time of reading.

Remember, I am addressing you as if you were a new convert. Here is your second way to encounter Christ. And this second way to Christ, although you will be using the Scripture, has a purpose altogether different from "praying the Scripture." For that reason you should set aside a separate time when you can come just to wait upon Him.

In "praying the Scripture" you are seeking to find the Lord in what you are reading, in the very words themselves. In this path, therefore, the content of the Scripture is the focal point of your attention. Your purpose is to take everything from the passage that unveils the Lord to you.

What of this second path?

In "beholding the Lord," you come to the Lord in a totally different way. Perhaps at this point I need to share with you the greatest difficulty you will have in waiting upon the Lord. It has to do with your mind. The mind has a very strong tendency to stray away from the Lord. Therefore, as you come before your Lord to sit in His presence, beholding Him, make use of the Scripture *to quiet your mind.*

The way to do this is really quite simple.

First, read a passage of Scripture. Once you sense the Lord's presence, the content of what you have read is no longer important. The Scripture has served its purpose; it has quieted your mind; it has brought you to Him.

So that you can see this more clearly, let me describe the way in which you come to the Lord by the simple act of beholding Him and waiting upon Him.

You begin by setting aside a time to be with the Lord. When you do come to Him, come quietly. Turn your heart to the presence of God. How is this done? This, too, is quite simple. You turn to Him by *faith*. By faith you believe you have come into the presence of God.

Next, while you are before the Lord, begin to read some portion of Scripture.

As you read, *pause*.

The pause should be quite gentle. You have paused so that you may set your mind on the Spirit. You have set your mind *inwardly*—on Christ.

(You should always remember that you are not doing this to gain some understanding of what you have read; rather, you are reading in order to turn your mind from outward things to the deep parts of your being. You are not there to learn or to read, but you are there to experience the presence of your Lord!)

While you are before the Lord, hold your heart in His presence. How? This you also do by faith. Yes, by faith you can hold your heart in the Lord's presence. Now, waiting before Him, turn all your attention toward your spirit. Do not allow your mind to wander. If your mind begins to wander, just turn your attention back again to the inward parts of your being.

You will be free from wandering—free from any outward distractions—and you will be brought near to God.

(The Lord is found *only* within your spirit, in the recesses of your being, in the Holy of Holies; this is where He dwells. The Lord once promised to come and make His home within you. (John 14:23) He promised to there meet those who worship Him and who do His will. The Lord *will* meet you in your spirit. It was St. Augustine who once said that he had lost much time in the beginning of his Christian experience by trying to find the Lord outwardly rather than by turning inwardly.)

Once your heart has been turned inwardly to the Lord, you will have an impression of His presence. You will be able to notice His presence more acutely because your outer senses have now become very calm and quiet. Your attention is no longer on outward things or on the surface thoughts of your mind; instead, sweetly and silently, your mind becomes occupied with what you have read and by that touch of His presence.

Oh, it is not that you will think about what you have read, but you will *feed* upon what you have read. Out of a love for the Lord you exert your will to hold your mind quiet before Him.

When you have come to this state, you must allow your mind to rest.

How shall I describe what to do next?

In this very peaceful state, *swallow* what you have tasted. At first this may seem difficult, but perhaps I can show you just how simple it is. Have you not, at times, enjoyed the flavor of a very tasty food? But unless you were willing to swallow the food, you received no nourishment. It is the same with your soul. In this quiet, peaceful, and simple state, simply take in what is there as nourishment.

What about distractions?

Let us say your mind begins to wander. Once you have been deeply touched by the Lord's Spirit and are distracted, be diligent to bring your wandering mind back to the Lord. This is the easiest way in the world to overcome external distractions.

When your mind has wandered, don't try to deal with it by changing what you are thinking. You see, if you pay attention to what you are thinking, you will only irritate your mind and stir it up more. Instead, *withdraw* from your mind! Keep turning within to the Lord's presence. By doing this you will win the war with your wandering mind and yet never directly engage in the battle!

Before we close this chapter, I would like to bring up one or two more points.

Let us talk about divine revelation. In the past, your reading habit may have been to wander from one subject to another. But the best way to *understand* the mysteries that are hidden in the revelation of God *and* to *enjoy* them fully is to let them be imprinted deeply in your heart. How? You may do this by dwelling on that revelation just as long as it gives you a sense of the Lord. Do not be quick to go from one thought to another. Stay with what *the Lord* has revealed to you; stay there just as long as a sense of the Lord is also there.

As you begin this new venture you will, of course, discover that it is difficult to bring your mind under control. Why is this? Because through many years of habit your mind has acquired the ability to wander all over the world, just as it pleases; so what I speak of here is something that is to serve as a discipline to your mind.

Be assured that as your soul becomes more accustomed to withdrawing to inward things, this process will become much easier.

There are two reasons that you will find it easier each time to bring your mind under subjection to the Lord. One is that the mind, after much practice, will form a new habit of turning deep within. The second is that you have a gracious Lord!

The Lord's chief desire is to reveal Himself to you and, in order for Him to do that, He gives you abundant grace. The Lord gives you the experience of enjoying His presence. He touches you, and His touch is so delightful that, more than ever, you are drawn inwardly to Him.

3

The Depths—Even for the Unlearned

I would like to address this chapter to those of you who may not be able to read.* Because you cannot read, you may feel that you are in a weaker state than most Christians. You may feel you are unqualified to know the depths of your Lord. But in fact, you are really blessed. The blessing in not being able to read is that *prayer* may become your reading! Do you not know that the greatest book is *Jesus Christ* Himself? He is a Book who has been written on within and without. He will teach you all things. Read Him!

The first thing you must learn, dear friend, is that "the kingdom of God is within you."(Luke 17:21)

Never look for the kingdom anywhere but *there,* within. Once you have realized that the kingdom of God is within you and can be found there, just come to the Lord.

As you come, come with a deep sense of *love;* come to Him very *gently;* come to Him with a deep sense of

---

*If you can read, don't skip this chapter because you will still be greatly helped! Please remember that until the last century a great majority of the world's population could not read. Jeanne Guyon has addressed herself to them. If this book is being read to one who cannot read, it will prove *most* helpful.

G.E.

worship. As you come to Him, humbly acknowledge that He is everything. Confess to Him that you are nothing.

Close your eyes to everything around you; begin to open the inward eyes of your soul, turning those eyes to your spirit. In a word, give your full attention to the deep inward parts of your being.

You need only believe that God dwells in you. This belief, and this belief alone, will bring you into His holy presence. Do not allow your mind to wander about but hold it in submission as much as possible.

Once you are in the Lord's presence, be still and quiet before Him.

And now, there in His presence, simply begin to repeat the Lord's Prayer. Begin with the word, "Father." As you do, let the full meaning of that word deeply touch your heart. Believe that the God who lives inside you is indeed so willing to be your Father. Pour out your heart to Him as a little child pours out his heart to his father. *Never* doubt your Lord's deep love for you. *Never* doubt His desire to hear you. Call on His name and remain before Him silently for a little while. Remain there, waiting to have His heart made known to you.

As you come to Him, come as a weak child, one who is all soiled and badly bruised—a child that has been hurt from falling again and again. Come to the Lord as one who has no strength of his own; come to Him as one who has no power to cleanse himself. Humbly lay your pitiful condition before your Father's gaze.

While you wait there before Him, occasionally utter a word of love to Him and a word of grief over your sin. Then simply wait for a while. After waiting, you will sense when it is time to go on; when that moment comes, simply continue on in the Lord's Prayer.

As you speak the words, "Thy Kingdom come." call upon your Lord, the King of Glory, to reign in you.

Give yourself up to God. Give yourself to God so that *He* may do in your heart what you have so long been a failure in trying to do.

Acknowledge before Him His right to rule over you.

At some point in this encounter with your Lord, you will feel deep within your spirit that it is time to simply remain silent before Him. When you have such a sense, do not move on to the next word—not as long as this sense continues with you. You see, it is the Lord Himself who is holding you to silence. When that sense of waiting before Him has passed, go on again to the next words of the Lord's Prayer.

"Your will be done on earth as it is in heaven."

Praying these words, humble yourself before the Lord, earnestly asking Him to accomplish His whole will in you and through you. Surrender your heart into His hands. Surrender your freedom into His hands. Yield to your Lord His right to do with you as He pleases.

Do you know what God's will is?

His will is that His children love Him. Therefore, when you pray, "Lord, Your will be done," you are actually asking the Lord to allow you to *love* Him. So begin to love Him! And as you do, beseech Him to give you His love.

All that I have just described to you will take place

very sweetly, and it will take place very peacefully, throughout the entire prayer.

Let us look now at another possibility.

There may come an occasion while you are with the Lord that you will wish to lay aside the Lord's Prayer. Perhaps you will wish to come to Him as your *shepherd.*

Come to Him, then, as a sheep who is looking to his shepherd for his *real* food. As you come to Him, utter something like this: "Oh, loving Shepherd, You feed Your flock with Yourself, and You are really my daily bread."

It is proper for you to bring all your needs to your Lord. But whatever you do, do it believing one thing; that is, that God is found within you.

I realize that you might be one of those who has a set pattern, or ritual, to your prayers. You should not burden yourself with the rituals you have learned. There is no need for using repetition or memorized prayers. Instead, simply repeat the Lord's Prayer as I have here described. It will produce abundant fruit in your life.

Dear child of God, all your concepts of what God is like really amount to nothing. Do not try to imagine what God is like. Instead, simply believe in His presence.Never try to imagine what God will do. There is no way God will ever fit into your concepts. What then shall you do? Seek to behold Jesus Christ by looking to Him in your inmost being, in your spirit.

Let us close this chapter by looking at a third way in which you may begin a deeper encounter with your Lord.

You may come to the Lord by looking to Him as your Physician. Bring to Him all your sicknesses so that He can heal them. But as you come to Him, do not come with anxiety or restlessness. And as you come, pause from time to time. This period of waiting silently before the Lord will gradually *increase*! Furthermore, your own efforts at praying will grow less and less. Eventually there will come for you that moment when He will gain complete control, when you will continually yield to God's working within you.

As you can see, what has begun as something very simple *will* grow! It will grow to become a very real and vital relationship between you and the living God.

When the presence of the Lord really becomes your experience, you will actually discover that you have gradually begun to love this silence and peaceful rest which come with His presence.

There is a wonderful enjoyment of His presence.

This wonderful enjoyment of His presence will now help introduce you to yet another *level* of prayer!

We will go on to this second level of prayer in the next chapter. It is a depth of prayer that can be experienced by all believers, the simple as well as the scholarly.

4*

The Second Level

You now have some acquaintance with *praying the Scripture* and *beholding the Lord* or *waiting in His presence.* Let us assume that you have practiced these two ways of coming to the Lord. Let us say that you have passed through the awkward stage of this and have come into real experience.

Now let us move on to consider a deeper level of experience with the Lord; that is, a deeper level of prayer. Some have described this second level as an experience of "faith and stillness." Others have referred to it as the "prayer of simplicity." I prefer the latter name.

Let us say you have grown accustomed to praying the Scripture and to waiting quietly in the sense of the Lord's presence, that these have made themselves part of your life. If this is so, you have found that it is now much easier to come to the Lord and to know His presence. But I would like to remind you once more that

*I am aware, dear reader, that nothing is going to stop you from reading all the way through this book; nonetheless, Chapter 4 is written for you to read after a strong foundation has been established in Chapters 1-3. And that should take a good while.

G.E.

what was written previously was written *to those who are just beginning to know Christ.*

When you first began, it was very difficult for you to recall your wandering mind. It was difficult to continually turn inward to your spirit. Little by little, these matters have become much more natural and simple. And now prayer has come to be easy, sweet, and natural—as well as very delightful. You gradually recognize that prayer is the true way, the *real* way, of finding God. And once you have found Him, you proclaim joyfully, "His name is an ointment poured forth." (Song of Solomon 1:3)

You might think that I would now encourage you to continue on in this very successful path. Instead, I am going to encourage you to change your course just a little. In so doing, once more you are going to come to a point that might have some discouragement in it. Starting out on a new path to explore the Lord always means encountering some difficulties at the outset! Therefore, I would encourage you to have a believing heart from this point on. You *must not* be discouraged. There *will* be a little difficulty along the way as you seek to go into a deeper relationship with the Lord.

Now with these words behind us, let us look at this new level of prayer.

First of all, come into the Lord's presence by faith. As you are there before Him, keep turning inward to your spirit until your mind is collected and you are perfectly still before Him. Now, when all your attention is finally turned within and your mind is set on the Lord, simply remain quiet before Him for a little while.

Perhaps you will begin to enjoy a sense of the Lord's presence. If that is the case, *do not try to think* of anything. Do not try to *say* anything. Do not try to *do* anything! As long as the sense of the Lord's presence continues, *just remain there.* Remain before Him exactly as you are.

The awareness of His presence will eventually begin to decrease. When this happens, utter some words of love to the Lord or simply call on His name. Do this quietly and gently with a believing heart. In so doing, you will once again be brought back to the sweetness of His presence! You will discover that you once more return to that sweet place of utter enjoyment that you have just experienced! Once the sweetness of His presence has returned to its fullest, *again* be still before Him.

You should not seek to move as long as He is near.

What is the point? The point is this: There is a fire within you and it ebbs and grows. That fire, when it ebbs, must be gently fanned, but *only* gently. Just as soon as that fire begins to burn, again *cease all* your efforts. Otherwise, you might put out the flame.

This, then, is the second level of prayer—a second level in experiencing Jesus Christ.

When you have come to the end of this time, always remain there before the Lord, quietly, for a little while. Also, it is very important that all of your prayer be done with a believing heart. Praying with a believing heart is more important than *anything else* that has to do with prayer!

Before we finish this chapter, I would like to talk with you just a moment about the motive of your heart in your seeking the Lord.

After all, why *do* you come to the Lord? Do you

come to Him for the sweetness? Do you come to Him because it is enjoyable to be in the Lord's presence? Let me recommend a higher way.

As you come to the Lord to pray, bring a full heart of pure love, a love that is not seeking anything for itself. Bring a heart that is seeking nothing *from* the Lord, but desires only to please Him and to do His will.

Let me illustrate. Consider the servant. The servant takes good care of His master; but if he does it only to receive some reward, he is not worthy of any consideration whatsoever. So, dear Christian, as you come to your Lord to pray, do not come for spiritual enjoyment. Do not even come to experience your Lord.

Then what? Come just to *please* Him.

Once you are there, if He chooses to pour out some great blessing, receive it. But if, instead, your mind wanders, receive *that*. Or if you have a difficult time in prayer, receive that. Joyfully accept whatever He desires to give. Believe that whatever happens is what *He* wants to give you!

Let me repeat that, for it is very important! It is especially important to you for any future growth in experiencing Christ. Believe by faith that whatever happens is His desire for you at that time.

When you have come to the Lord *this* way, you will find that your spirit is at peace no matter what your condition. When you have learned to come to the Lord with this attitude, you will not be upset if the Lord withdraws Himself from you. The times of spiritual dryness will be the same to you as the times of spiritual abundance. You will treat them both the same. Why? Because you will have learned to love God just because you love Him, not because of His gifts, *nor even for His precious presence.*

5

Periods of Dryness

In chapter four we touched on the subject of spiritual "dry spells." If you set forth for the spiritual lands that have been described in these first chapters, you must realize that times of dryness await you. It would be wise of us, then, to continue this subject for just a little while longer.

Dear reader, you must realize that God has only one desire. Certainly you can never understand a dry spell unless you understand what His desire is. His desire is to give Himself to the soul that really loves Him and to that soul which earnestly seeks Him. *And yet* it is true that this God who desires to give Himself to you will often conceal Himself from you—from you, the very one who seeks Him!

Now why would God do that? Dear saint of God, you must learn the ways of your Lord. Yours is a God who often hides Himself. He hides Himself for a purpose. Why? *His purpose is to rouse you from spiritual laziness.* His purpose in removing Himself from you is to cause you to pursue Him.

The Lord Jesus is looking about everywhere for that Christian who will remain faithful and loving even when He has withdrawn Himself. If the Lord finds such a faithful soul, when He does return, He rewards the faithfulness of His child. He pours out upon that faithful one abundant goodness and tender caresses of love.

Here, then, is something you must understand.

You *will* have times of spiritual dryness. It is part of the Lord's way.

But the fact you will have spiritual dry spells is *not* the issue. The important question is what you will *do* in a time of spiritual dryness? At this point you must learn something about your natural tendencies. It will be the natural thing for you, during a dry season, to try to *prove* your love to the Lord. During a spiritually dry season you will find that you will try to prove to the Lord your faithfulness toward Him; you will do this by exerting your strength. Unconsciously you will be hoping by such self effort to persuade Him to return more quickly.

No, dear Christian, believe me, this is not the way to respond to your Lord in seasons of dryness.

What then shall you do?

You must await the return of your Beloved with *patient love.* Join with that love *self denial* and *humiliation*! Even though the Lord has hidden Himself, remain constantly before Him. There before Him, pour out your love upon Him passionately and yet, I would add, always peacefully.

Spend time with Him in worship and in respectful silence.

By waiting upon the Lord in this way, you will demonstrate to Him that it is He alone whom you are seeking. You see, you will be demonstrating that it is not the selfish enjoyment which you receive from being in His presence that causes you to love Him. You will be showing that it is not the pleasure which you experience, *but your love* that motivates you.

There is a quotation from the Apocrypha that speaks of such seasons:

> *Do not be impatient in times of dryness and darkness; allow the removals and delays of the consolations of God; draw near to Him and wait upon Him patiently that your life may be increased and be renewed.*

So, dear children of the Lord, be patient in your prayer during those seasons of dryness.

Let me ask you a question. What if the Lord called upon you to spend *your whole lifetime* waiting for His return to you? How would you conduct yourself if this were the lot the Lord should mete out to you for all the rest of your life? What *would* you do?

Do this.

Wait upon Him in a spirit of humility, in a spirit of abandonment, with contentment and resignation. Spend your time in that wonderful kind of prayer which I have mentioned in Chapter 4. Come before Him quietly and peacefully, recalling your mind to His presence even though His presence may evade you.

As you do these things, accompany them all with pleas of sorrowful, plaintive love and expressions of yearnings for your lover's return.

I wish to assure you that if you will conduct yourself *this way*, it will please the heart of God greatly. Such an attitude will compel Him to return to you much more quickly than any other.

6

Abandonment

At the outset of this book we discussed how to know the depths of Jesus Christ. Our beginning was quite simple. We looked first at *praying the Scripture* and then at the simplicity of just *beholding the Lord.* After you have pursued this level of experience with the Lord for a *considerable* length of time, you then should be ready to go on to a deeper level of experience with Him and a deeper level of knowing Him. But in this deeper encounter with the Lord which we looked at in Chapter 4, you must move outside the realm of prayer alone; or, to state it more clearly, you must move away from just that one or two times a day you set apart for prayer with the Lord.

At this point, there must enter into your heart whole new attitudes toward your entire life. If you are to branch out beyond just a time of prayer each day, other parts of your life—and even your whole viewpoint of life—will have to be altered. This new attitude must come for a very special reason—so that you may go on deeper, still deeper, into another level with your Lord.

To do this, you must have a fresh attitude toward yourself as well as toward the Lord; it is an attitude that must go much deeper than any you have known previously.

To do this, I introduce a new word to you. The word is *abandonment*.

To penetrate deeper in the experience of Jesus Christ, it is required that you begin to abandon your whole existence, giving it up to God. Let us take the daily occurrences of life as an illustration. You must utterly believe that the circmstances of your life, that is, every minute of your life, as well as the whole course of your life—anything, yes, *everything* that happens—have all come to you by His will and by His permission. You must utterly believe that everything that has happened to you is from God and is exactly what you need.

Do you remember in an earlier chapter that you saw how you could first be introduced to such a disposition? You can begin by accepting every time of prayer, whether it be a glorious time with Him or a time when your mind wanders, as being exactly what He desired for you. Then learn to broaden this perspective until it encompasses *every* second of your life!

Such an outlook towards your circumstances and such a look of faith towards your Lord will make you *content* with *everything*. Once you believe this, you will then begin to take everything that comes into your life as being from the hand of God, not from the hand of man.

Do you truly, sincerely desire to give yourself up to God?

Then I must next remind you that once you have made the donation, you cannot take the gift back again. Once the gift has been presented, it no longer belongs to the giver. This little book is written to tell you how to experience the depths of Jesus Christ, but knowing the depths of Jesus Christ is not just a method. It is a life-long attitude. It is a matter of being enveloped by God and possessed by Him.

We have spoken of abandonment. Abandonment is a matter of the greatest importance if you are to make progress in knowing your Lord. Abandonment is, in fact, *the key* to the *inner court*—the key to the fathomless depths. Abandonment is the key to the inward spiritual life.

The believer who knows how to abandon himself to the Lord will soon become perfect.*

Let us say you reach this state of abandonment. Once you have reached this state, you must continue, steadfast and immovable. Otherwise, to arrive there and remain only briefly is of little value. It is one thing to reach this state; it is another thing to remain there.

Be careful; do not listen to the voice of your natural reasoning. You can expect just such reasoning to well up within you. Nonetheless, you must believe that *you can* abandon yourself utterly to the Lord for all your lifetime and that He will give you the grace to remain there! You must trust in God, "hoping against hope." (Romans 4:18)

Great faith produces great abandonment.

What is abandonment? If we can understand what it is, perhaps we can better lay hold of it.

Abandonment is casting off all your cares. Abandonment is dropping all your needs. This includes *spiritual* needs. Let me repeat that, for it is not easily

*Jeanne Guyon did not have in mind *sinless* perfection, but a life lived and a will lived in absolute, perfect concert with the will of God—constantly, under all circumstances, at all times.

G.E.

grasped. Abandonment is laying aside, forever, *all* of your spiritual needs.

All Christians *have* spiritual needs; but the believer who has abandoned himself to the Lord no longer indulges in the luxury of being aware of spiritual needs. Rather, he gives himself over completely to the disposal of God.

Do you realize that all Christians have been exhorted to abandonment?

The Lord Himself has said, "Take no thought for tomorrow, for your heavenly Father knows that you have need of all these things." (Matthew 6:32, 34) Again the Scripture says, "In all your ways acknowledge Him, and He will direct your paths." (Proverbs 3:6) "Commit your works unto the Lord, and your thoughts shall be established." (Proverbs 16:3) Again, in the book of Psalms it says, "Commit your ways to the Lord, trust also in Him, and He will bring it to pass." (Psalm 37:5)

True abandonment must cover two complete worlds, two complete realms.

There must be an abandonment in your life concerning all *outward,* practical things. Secondly, there must also be an abandonment of all *inward,* spiritual things. You must come to the Lord and there engage in giving up *all* your concerns. All your concerns go into the hand of God. You forget yourself, and from that moment on you think *only of Him.*

By continuing to do this over a long period of time, your heart will remain *unattached;* your heart will be free and at peace!

How do you practice abandonment? You practice it

daily, hourly, and by the moment. Abandonment is practiced by *continually* losing your own will in the will of God; by plunging your will into the depths of *His* will, there to be lost forever!

And how do you begin? You must begin by refusing every personal desire that comes to you just as soon as it arises—no matter how good that personal desire is, and no matter how helpful it might appear!

Abandonment must reach a point where you stand in complete indifference to yourself. You can be sure that out of such a disposition a wonderful result will come.

The result of this attitude will, in fact, bring you to the most wonderful point imaginable. It is the point where your will breaks free of you completely and becomes free to be joined to the will of God! You will desire only what He desires, that is, what He *has desired* for all eternity.

Become abandoned by simply resigning yourself to what the Lord wants, in all things, no matter what they are, where they come from, or how they affect your life.

What is abandonment? It is forgetting your past; it is leaving the future in His hands; it is devoting the present fully and completely to your Lord. Abandonment is being satisfied with the present moment, no matter what that moment contains. You are satisfied because you know that whatever that moment has, it contains—in that instant—God's eternal plan for you.

You will always know that that moment is the absolute and total *declaration* of His will for your life.

Remember, you must never blame man for anything. No matter what happens, it was neither man nor circumstances that brought it. You must accept everything (except, of course, your own sinfulness) as having come from your Lord.

Surrender not only what the Lord does to you, but surrender your *reaction* to what He does.

Do you wish to go into the depths of Jesus Christ? If you wish to enter into this deeper state of knowing the Lord, you must seek to know not only a deeper prayer but also abandonment in all realms of your life. This means branching out until your new relationship includes living 24 hours a day utterly abandoned to Him. Begin to surrender yourself to be led by God and to be dealt with by Him. Do so right now. Surrender yourself to allow Him to do with you exactly as He pleases—both in your *inward* life of experiencing Him and also in your *outward* life of accepting all circumstances as from Him.

7

Abandonment and Suffering

I would like to continue speaking with you about abandonment, but in this chapter let us see how such a consecration affects you when suffering comes into your life.

You must be patient in all the suffering that God sends you. If your love for the Lord is pure, you will love Him as much on Calvary as on Mt. Tabor. The Lord Jesus loved His Father on Mt. Tabor where He was transfigured, but He loved Him no less on Calvary where He was crucified. Surely, then, you should love the Lord as much on Calvary, for it was there that He made the greatest display of His love.

There is a possibility that you might make a mistake concerning your abandonment to the Lord. You may abandon yourself to the Lord hoping and expecting always to be carressed and loved and spiritually blessed by Him. You who have given yourself to the Lord during some pleasant season, please take note of this: If you gave yourself to Him to be *blessed* and to be *loved,* you cannot suddenly turn around and take back your life at another season . . . when you are being *crucified*!

Nor will you find any comfort from man when you have been put on the cross. Any comfort that comes to you when you are knowing the cross comes to you from the Lord.

You must learn to love the cross. He who does not love the cross does not love the things of God. (Matthew 16:23) It is impossible for you to truly love the Lord without loving the cross. The believer who loves the cross finds that even the bitterest things that come his way are sweet. The Scripture says, "To the hungry soul every bitter thing is sweet." (Proverbs 27:7)

How much do you desire to hunger after God? You will hunger after God, and find Him, in the same proportion that you hunger after the cross.

Here is a true spiritual principle that the Lord will not deny: God gives us the cross, and then the cross gives us God.

As you can see, now we have moved outside the realm of a certain period of time set aside for prayer; we have now moved into a realm that involves the whole experience of the believer. Let it be said here and now: You may be certain there will come to you an inward spiritual advancement when there is also in your life a real progress in knowing the experience of the cross. Abandonment to Christ and the experience of the cross go hand in hand.

Then how will you treat suffering? Or, to put it another way, how do you respond to the Lord's working of the cross in your life?

You respond this way. As soon as anything comes to you in the form of suffering, at that very moment a natural resistance will well up somewhere inside you. When that moment comes, immediately resign yourself to God. *Accept the matter.* In that moment give yourself up to Him as a sacrifice.

By doing this, you will eventually make a wonderful discovery. It is this: When the cross does arrive in your life, it will not be nearly as burdensome as you first feared. Receive it as from God, no matter what it is. The burden is far lighter this way.

Why is the cross so much lighter when accepted in this way? Because you will have *desired* the cross, and you will have accustomed yourself to receive everything from the hand of the Lord.

Do not misunderstand these words. I have not described to you a way to get out of the cross. Even though you utterly abandon yourself to the Lord and completely resign yourself to suffering, this will not prevent you from feeling the weight of that cross. If you have not felt the cross, then you have not suffered. Feeling the *pain* of suffering is one of the principal parts of suffering. Pain is an inescapable aspect of the cross. Without it, there has been no cross at all. Suffering is woven into the nature of the cross. Pain is at the center of knowing suffering. Please remember that your Lord chose to endure the most extreme violence the cross could offer.

Sometimes you may bear the cross in weakness; at other times you may bear the cross in strength. But whether you bear it in weakness or in strength, *bear it!* Both weakness and strength should be the same to us since we bear the cross in the will of God.

8

Abandonment And Revelation

Let us continue viewing this matter of abandonment.

Some have asked the question, "If I utterly abandon myself to the Lord, will that mean I will have no new revelation of Jesus Christ?"

Does abandonment end revelation?

No, it does not. Quite the contrary, abandonment is the means that the Lord will use to give you revelation. The revelation you receive will come to you as *reality* rather than *knowledge.* This is made possible *only* by abandonment.

You must remember *to whom* it is you are abandoning yourself.

It is to the Lord Jesus that you abandon yourself. It is also the Lord whom you will follow as the Way; it is this Lord that you will hear as the Truth, and it is from this Lord that you will receive Life. (John 14:6) If you follow Him as the Way, you will hear Him as the Truth, and He will bring life to you as the Life.

As revelation comes to you, something happens; Jesus Christ actually makes an imprint of Himself upon your soul. Each time He comes to you, He leaves a new and different impression of His nature upon you.

Soon there are many different expressions of His nature impressed into your being.

Perhaps you have heard that you should *think* on the different experiences of Jesus Christ. But it is far better for you to bear, to carry, these experiences of Jesus Christ *within* yourself.

This is the way it was in the life of Paul. He did not ponder the sufferings of Christ; he did not consider the marks of suffering on the Lord's body. Instead, Paul bore in his own body the experiences of his Lord. He even said, "I bear in my body the marks of Jesus Christ." (Galatians 6:17) Did he do so by considering such marks? No. Jesus Christ had personally imprinted Himself upon Paul.

When the Lord finds a believer who is completely abandoned to Him in all things *without* and in all things *within*, He will often choose to give that person special revelations of His nature. If such should be your experience, accept these revelations with a thankful heart.

Always receive everything from Him with a thankful heart, no matter what it is He chooses to bestow.

Let us say that the Lord gives you special revelation. What should be your attitude? You must receive the revelation as you would receive all other things from Him.

There are Christians to whom God has given some revelation of Himself, and that revelation has brought enjoyment to them for years. In other words, sometimes the Lord will give you such a powerful revelation of Himself that the experience of that one truth will be your strength for years. During that time you are drawn more and more inwardly to God. This is wonderful. You should be faithful to that revelation just as long as it lasts.

But what happens when that revelation begins to fade away; what do you do when it no longer brings the enjoyment it once did? When this happens, it simply means that God has decided it best to put an end to that experience. What must be your attitude? You must freely yield to having it taken away from you. Lay it aside. The Lord wishes to move on to a deeper and more central understanding of Himself. Receive all things equally. Abandon yourself even in matters of revelation. Always be ready to give yourself to whatever seems to be His will. Have no desire in your life except the desire to reach passionately after Him and to always dwell with Him. Learn what it means to continually sink into nothingness before your Lord.

Learn, having done this, to accept equally all His gifts, whether they are light or darkness. Treat fruitfulness and barrenness the same way.

Whether it be weakness or strength, sweetness or bitterness, temptation, distraction, pain, weariness, uncertainty or blessing, all should be received as equal from the Lord's hand. *None* of these should delay your course even for a moment.

One last word about revelation.

The Lord gives you some revelation that you are unable to understand. Do not be distressed; you have no reason to be concerned. Simply love the Lord. This love includes within itself every kind of devotion for Him. If you are one who is given up to God and God alone, then you will have no trouble seeing Jesus Christ revealed to you in all the fullness of His nature. Some part of the revelation of Himself may be very clear; some other part of that revelation may not be so clear.

Accept them both as the same. Anyone who loves God loves everything that pertains to Him. You joy in the revelation of Him that you do not understand just as you do in the revelation of Him that you do understand.

If you love Him, you love everything about Him.

9

Abandonment And a Holy Life

What is the result of walking continually before God in a state of abandonment? The ultimate result is godliness. Once you have made this relationship with God part of your life, godliness is easily within your reach.

What do we mean by godliness? Godliness is something that comes from God. If you are faithful to learn this simple way to experience your Lord, you will take possession of God. And as you possess Him, you will inherit all His traits. This is godliness: The more you possess God, the more you are made like Him.*

But it must be a godliness that has grown from *within* you. If godliness is not from deep within you, it is only a mask. The mere outward appearance of godliness is as changeable as a garment. But when godliness is produced in you from the Life that is deep within you—then that godliness is real, lasting, and the genuine essence of the Lord. "The King's daughter is all glorious within."(Psalm 45:13)

How, then, is godliness achieved?

The Christian who has learned to be abandoned to

*Transformation.

Jesus Christ and who walks in a life of abandonment to Him, practices godliness in the highest degree. But you would never hear such a person claim to possess any particular spirituality at all. Why? Because that Christian has become totally united with God. It is the Lord Himself who is leading that believer into this very thorough practice of godliness.

The Lord is very jealous over any saint who is utterly abandoned to Him. He does not let that believer have any pleasures at all outside of Himself.

Is abandonment the only thing necessary to bring us into godliness? No, but if you become faithful in following everything that has been said thus far, godliness *will* come. But do not forget that *suffering* is included in the experience of abandonment. It is the *fire* of suffering which will bring forth the *gold* of godliness.

Do not be fearful that you will not wish to walk this way. In the level of experience of which I now speak there is a hungering for suffering. Such Christians burn with love for the Lord. In fact, if they were permitted to follow their own desires, they would put themselves under a great deal of discipline, even excessive self-denial. Once such love burns within the heart of a believer, he thinks of nothing but how to please his beloved Lord. He begins to neglect himself—no, far more than that—in love with the Lord, he even completely *forgets* about himself. As his love for the Lord grows, so does his hatred for his self-life.

May you learn this path.

Oh, if this simple way to prayer, this simple experience of Jesus Christ, could be acquired by the Lord's children, the whole church of God would easily be reformed.

This way of prayer, this simple relationship to your Lord, is so suited for everyone; it is just as suited for the dull and the ignorant as it is for the well-educated. This prayer, this experience which begins so simply, has as its end a totally abandoned love to the Lord.

Only one thing is required—*love.*

St. Augustine said, "Love, then do what you please." For when you have learned to love, you will not even desire to do those things that might offend the One you love.

10

Living Indoors

In the last chapter we concluded by saying that the believer who is utterly in love with the Lord will not even desire the things that might offend the object of his affection. I will go on to say it is only by abandonment that it is possible to reach a *total* victory in subduing your *senses* and your *desires.*

Why is this so?

Actually, the reason is very obvious. First of all, you must understand the workings of your inmost parts. Where do your five senses draw their life and energy? From your soul. It is your soul that gives life and energy to your five senses; and when your *senses* become aroused, they in turn stimulate your *desires.*

How can we speak of a total victory over the five senses and over the passions and desire that become aroused through them?

If your body were dead, you would not be able to feel, and you certainly would have no desire. But why? Why would the body have no desire? Because it would be disconnected from the *soul.* So let me repeat, your feelings and your senses draw their power from the soul.

Christians have sought to find many ways to

overcome their desires. Perhaps the most common approach has been discipline and self-denial. But no matter how severe your self-denial may be, it will never completely conquer your senses.

No, self-denial is not the answer!

Even when it appears to have worked, what self-denial has actually done is to change only the *outward expression* of those desires.

When you deal with the externals, what you are really doing is driving your soul farther outward from your spirit. The more your soul is focused on these outward things, the farther it is removed from its *center* and from its resting place! The result of this type of self-denial is the opposite of what you sought. Unfortunately, this is what always happens to a believer when his life is lived out on the surface.

If you dwell on the desires of your outward nature—paying attention to them—they, in turn, become more and more active. Instead of being subdued, they gain more power. We can conclude from all this that although self-denial may truly weaken the body, it can *never* take away the keenness of your senses.

Then what is your hope?

There is only one way to conquer your five senses, and that is by inward recollection. Or, to put it another way, the only way to conquer your five senses is by turning your soul completely inward to your spirit, there to possess a *present* God. Your soul must turn all of its attention and energies *within*, not without! Within to Christ, not without to the senses. When your soul is turned within, it actually becomes *separated* from your external senses; and once your five senses are separated from your soul, they receive no more attention. Their life supply is cut off!

They become powerless.

Now let us follow the course of the soul. Your soul has learned at this point to turn within and draw near to the presence of God. The soul becomes farther and farther separated from the self. You may experience being powerfully drawn within—to seek God in your spirit—and discover that the outer man becomes very weak. (Some may even be prone to faintings.)

Your main concern, therefore, is with the presence of Jesus Christ. Your main concern lies in dwelling continually upon the God who is within you. Then, without particularly thinking of self-denial or "putting away the deeds of the flesh," God will cause you to experience a natural subduing of the flesh! You can be sure of this: The Christian who has faithfully abandoned himself to the Lord will soon discover that he also has laid hold of a God who will not rest until *He* has subdued everything! Your Lord will put to death all that remains to be put to death in your life.

What, then, is required of you? All you need to do is remain steadfast in giving your utmost attention to God. *He* will do all things perfectly. The truth is, not everyone is capable of severe outward self-denial, but *everyone* is capable of turning within and abandoning himself wholly to God.

It is true that what you see and what you hear are continually supplying your busy imagination with new subjects. They keep your thoughts jumping from one subject to another. Therefore, there is a place for discipline concerning what you see and hear. But be at peace; God will teach you about all this. All you need do is follow His Spirit.

Two great advantages will come to you if you proceed in the way I have described in this chapter. First of all, by withdrawing from outward objects, you will constantly draw nearer to God.

The closer you are to God, the more you receive His nature.

The more you receive His nature, the more you will draw upon His sustaining power.

Secondly, the nearer you draw to the Lord, the farther you are removed from sin. So you see, by simply turning within to your spirit, you begin to acquire the habit of being near to the Lord and far from all else.

11

Toward the Center

In the last chapter we discussed dealing with the outward senses. Here was our conclusion: If at any time you find your desires stirred up, those senses can best be deadened by a gentle retreat inward to a present God. Any other way of opposing your restless senses will merely stimulate them further.

As you come into this deeper level of knowing the Lord, you will eventually come to discover a principle I will call the *law of central tendency.*

What do I mean by the law of central tendency? As you continue holding your soul deep in your inward parts, you will discover that God has a *magnetic* attracting quality! Your God is like a magnet! The Lord naturally draws you more and more toward Himself.

The next thing you notice is this: As you move toward the center, the Lord also *purifies* you of all the things that are not of Him.

This is illustrated in nature. Observe the ocean. The water in the ocean begins to evaporate. Then the vapor begins moving toward the sun. As the vapor leaves the earth, it is full of impurities; however, as it ascends, it becomes more refined and more purified.

What did the vapor do?

The vapor did nothing. It simply *remained passive.* The purifying took place as the vapor was drawn up into the heavens!

There is one difference between your soul and those vapors. Although the vapor can *only* be passive, you have the privilege of cooperating *voluntarily* with the Lord as He draws you inwardly toward Himself.

When your soul is once turned toward God—the God who dwells within your spirit—you will find it easy to keep turning within. The longer you continue to turn within, the closer you will come to God and the more firmly you will cling to Him.

Of course, the closer you are drawn to God, the farther you are removed from the activities of your natural man. The natural man, to be sure, is very opposed to your inward drawing toward God. Nonetheless, there will come a point when you will finally be established in having turned within. From that point on, it will be natural for you to live before the Lord! In the past it was natural for you to live on the *surface* of your being; now it will be your habit to live in the *center* of your being where your Lord dwells.

May I remind you that you are like the vapors ascending to the heavens; you must not think that you can bring all this about by exerting *your* efforts. The only thing you can do—actually the only thing you should attempt to do—is to *keep withdrawing* yourself from *external* objects. Keep turning from external objects and keep turning within to your spirit. There is very little you should *ever* do, but that one thing you can do! Yes, you are capable of that much cooperation with divine grace.

Beyond that, though, you have nothing more to do but to continue firmly holding on to your Lord.

At the outset of this venture, all this may seem somewhat difficult to you; but be assured that this kind of inward turning becomes very easy. You will advance spiritually very naturally and effortlessly.

Again, this is because God has a magnetic attraction. He is within you, always drawing you to Himself.

You can see this principle in the natural elements. The center of anything always exerts a very powerful drawing force. That fact is even *more* true in the spiritual realm. On the one hand, there is a drawing force in the center of your being; it is powerful and irresistible. And on the other hand, there is also a very strong tendency in every man to be reunited to his center. The center is not only drawing the object away from the surface, but the object itself *tends* toward its center!

As you become more perfected in Christ, this tendency to be drawn within to the Lord becomes stronger and more active.

What might slow down the process of this *central tendency?*

Only some obstacle which stands between the outer object (you) and the inward magnet (Christ). As soon as anything turns toward its center, it will rush there very rapidly unless it is hindered.

Take, for instance, a stone. When you drop a stone from your hand, what does it do? It immediately falls to that earth from whence it once came. The stone returns to its original source. The same is true of fire and water. They always seek to return to their centers.

Your soul, once it begins to turn inward, is brought under this same law of central tendency. It too gradually falls toward its proper center, which is God. The soul needs no other force to draw it than the weight of love.

The more passive and peaceful you remain, the more quickly you will advance toward God. The freer you are from exerting your own effort, the more quickly you will move toward your Lord.

Why is this? Because there is a divine energy drawing you. When this divine energy is completely unhindered, *He* has complete liberty to draw you just as He pleases.

Jesus Christ is the great magnet of your soul, but of your soul only. He will not draw the impurities and mixtures that are mingled with it. Any such impurities prevent His full power of attraction.

If there were no mixture in your soul, the soul would instantly rush toward the all-powerful, irresistible God within to be lost in Him. But if you are loaded down with many material possessions—or anything else—this attraction is greatly hindered. Many Christians seize some part of this world or some part of the self with so tight a grip that they spend their whole lives making only a snail's progress toward their Center.

Thank God, sometimes your Lord, out of His boundless love, strikes the burden violently from your hand. It is then that you realize just how very much you had been hindered and held back. Dear Christian, only allow everything to drop. How? Simply withdraw your hands from self; withdraw your hands from every other person and all things. Of course, that is something of a sacrifice. It can even be called a crucifixion. But you will be amazed to find that there is only a very short space between your sacrifice and your resurrection!

Is it proper for the soul to become so completely passive?

Some seem to feel that, according to what I have said, the soul is required to become dead—dead like some lifeless object—before God has His will in it. Actually, the very opposite is true.

The main element of the soul is the *will*, and the soul must *will* to become neutral and passive, waiting entirely upon God. Can you not see that this condition of utter passivity, this state of doing nothing and waiting upon God, is actually the *highest* activity of the will? Listen to your soul as it says, "I am *willing* with all the power of my being that the desire of God be accomplished within me. I am *willing* to be here, ceasing from all my activity and all of my power, so that God might have His desire of fully possessing me."

When the soul has done this, it has actually exerted the highest possible action of the will. The soul has taken the action of total *surrender* to another will, the Divine Will!

Therefore, dear reader, give all your attention to learning how to turn within and dwell in your spirit. Do not be discouraged by any difficulties you may have encountered this far. Before long, God will give you abundant grace, and all this will be easy.

I would add only one admonition. You must remain faithful in humbly withdrawing your heart from outward distractions and occupations. Form the habit of continually returning to God, who is your center, with a peaceful, tender love.

12

Continual Prayer

If you remain faithful in the things touched on up until now, you will be astonished to feel the Lord gradually taking possession of your whole being. I would like to remind you that this book was not written for your enjoyment. Neither is it presenting just some method of prayer. The purpose of this book is to offer a way in which the Lord Jesus *can take full possession of you.*

As the Lord gradually begins to do this, to take full possession of you, it is true that you will begin to enjoy a sense of His presence. You will find that this sense of the Lord's presence will become very natural to you. Both the prayer with which you first began and a sense of His presence *which comes with that prayer,* will eventually become a normal part of your daily experience.

An unusual serenity and peacefulness will gradually spread over your soul. Your whole prayer, your whole experience, will begin to enter upon a new level.

What is this new level? It is prayer. Prayer that consists of silence. And while in this silence, God pours into you a deep, inward love. This experience of love is one that will fill and permeate your whole being. There is no way to describe this experience, this encounter. I would only say that this love which the Lord pours into your depths is the beginning of an indescribable blessedness.

I wish it were possible in this little book to tell you some of the levels of endless experiences you can have with the Lord, experiences that come out of this encounter with God. But I must remember that this little book is written for beginners. Therefore, I trust on some future day I will be able to relate these deeper experiences to you.

There is one thing I will say, however. When you come to the Lord, gradually learn to have a quiet mind before Him. One of the most important things you can do is cease from any self-effort. In this way, God Himself can act all alone. It was the Psalmist speaking for the Lord who said, "Be still and know that I am God." (Psalm 46:10)

This verse gives you an insight into your own mind. Your self nature becomes so pleasantly attached to its own efforts that it simply cannot believe that anything is going on within your spirit. Unless the mind is able to feel and understand, it refuses to believe the spirit is having experience.

The reason you are sometimes unable to *feel* God's working within you is that the work is fully within the realm of the spirit, and not in the mind. Sometimes God's workings in you are quite rapid, and yet the mind is not even aware that you are making progress. The workings of God in you, always increasing more and more, are absorbing the workings of your self.

Let me illustrate this.

During the night the stars shine very brightly, but as the sun begins to come up, the stars gradually vanish.

Actually the stars are still there; they have not stopped shining; but the sun is so much brighter that you cannot see them. The same is true in spiritual matters. There is a strong and universal light which absorbs all the smaller lights of your soul. The smaller lights of your soul grow fainter and eventually disappear under the powerful light of your Spirit. Self activity is no longer able to be distinguished or noticed.

Self-effort becomes swallowed up in the working of God.

Sometimes the question is raised, "Is not this prayer experience one of inactivity?" The question would not even be asked if it were preceded by experience. If you will make some effort to obtain this experience of prayer, this deeper experience with Jesus Christ, you will be full of light and understanding concerning the state of your soul. No, the soul is not inactive—at least not because of barrenness or lack—but has become *still* because of great abundance.

The Christian who has laid hold of this encounter will understand this and will recognize that this *silence* is rich, full, and alive! This silence is coming forth from a storehouse of plenty!

You see, there are two kinds of people who keep silent. The first is one who has nothing to say, and the other is one who has too much to say. In the case of this deeper encounter with the Lord, the latter is true. Silence is produced from excess, not from lack. To die of thirst is one thing; to be drowned is quite another. Yet water causes both. In one, it is a lack of water, and in the other, too much water causes death.

This experience with Christ has its beginning in a simple way to pray. Gradually, though, it goes on from there. The experience deepens until the fullness of grace completely stills the activity of the self. Therefore, you see why it is of the greatest importance that you remain as quieted as possible.

May I illustrate this again? When a baby is born, it draws milk from its mother's breast by moving its lips. However, once the milk begins to flow, the child simply swallows without any further effort. If the baby continued any effort, it would hurt itself, spill the milk, and have to quit nursing.

This must be your attitude in prayer. You must act this same way, especially in the beginning. Draw ever so gently. But as the Lord flows out of your spirit into your soul, cease all activity.

How do you begin? By moving your lips, by stirring up the affections of your love for the Lord. As soon as the milk of divine love is flowing freely, be still—do nothing. Rather, very simply and sweetly, take in that grace and love. When this grace, this sense of the Lord's love, ceases to flow, it is time once again to stir up your affections. How? Just as the infant does by moving its lips.

All this time remain very quiet. If you bring yourself to the Lord in some other way, you will not make the best use of this grace. You see, the sense of the Lord's presence has been given to you, by the Lord, to allure you into a restful experience of love. It goes without saying that His presence has not been given to you to stir up an activity of the self.

Let us return to the illustration of the nursing baby.

Let us say the baby has drunk gently of the milk and has done so completely without effort. Now what happens? You would have to admit that all of us find it hard to believe that we could receive nourishment in such a passive way, as a baby receives his. And yet, look at the baby: the more peacefully it nurses, the better it thrives. So I will ask the question again: What becomes of the little baby after it has nursed?

It falls asleep on its mother's breast.

It is the same way with your soul. When the Christian has become calm and peaceful in prayer, he frequently sinks into a sort of mystical sleep; or to put it another way, the powers of his soul are completely at rest.

It is here, at this point, that you begin to be introduced to yet a deeper level of experience.

The Christian now begins to touch on *an experience of complete rest* before the Lord.

The mind is at rest; the soul is at rest; the whole being has come to a gentle, quiet and peaceful calm before the Lord. Nothing disturbs it. At first you will experience this only occasionally, but eventually your soul will come to experience this state of rest frequently.

Be sure of this: Your soul will be led into this experience without effort, without trouble, and without skill. And all you need to do is to continue with the Lord each day, waiting for Him to deepen your experience with Him

Let us look closer at what has just been said.

The interior life, that is, the inward life of the spirit, is not a place that is taken by storm or violence. That inward kingdom, that realm within you, is a place of peace. It can only be gained by love.

If you will simply pursue the path I have pointed out until now, you will be led to this quiet place of rest.

And beyond this rest lies yet another experience—that of *continual prayer.*

When we speak of continual prayer, we are speaking of a prayer that originates from within. It originates there and works out, filling and permeating your whole being. Nor is this a difficult matter. Actually, God demands nothing extraordinary. On the contrary, He is very pleased by a simple, childlike conduct.

I would even put it this way: The highest spiritual attainments are really the ones that are the most easily reached. The things that are most important are the things that are the least difficult!

Again, this can also be illustrated in nature.

Let us say that you wish to reach the sea. How will you get there? You need to do nothing except this: embark upon a river. Eventually you will be carried to the sea without any trouble, without any self-effort.

Now would you like to go into God? Then return to the early thoughts that we presented at the beginning of this little book. Follow this sweet and simple path. Continue on it, and eventually you will arrive at your desired object. You will arrive at God and with a speed never imagined.

Then what is lacking? Nothing! You need only to make the trial effort.

If you will make that initial effort, you will find that what I have said is really far too little to express the discovery that lies ahead. Your own experience with Jesus Christ will carry you infinitely beyond even *this* level.

What is there for you to fear? Dear child of God, why do you not instantly cast yourself into the arms of Love?

The only reason He extended those arms on the cross was so He might embrace you. Tell me, what possible risk do you take in depending solely upon God? What risk do you run by abandoning yourself completely to Him? The Lord will not deceive you (that is, unless it is to bestow on you more abundance than you ever imagined).

However, those who expect all of these things from the Lord by *self-effort* will hear the Lord's rebuke: "You have wearied yourselves in the multiplicity of your ways, and have not said, Let us rest in peace." (Isaiah 57:10)

13

Abundance

In the last chapter, we spoke of entering into a deeper level of experience with Jesus Christ.

At the very outset of this journey, you found that the only preparation you needed was a quiet waiting before God. The same is true in this new level of experience. This is no longer a rare experience, nor an occasional experience; gradually it becomes your *daily* experience. The presence of God begins to be poured forth within you. Eventually it will become yours almost without intermission.

In the beginning, you were led into His presence by prayer; but now, as prayer continues, the *prayer* actually *becomes* His presence. In fact, we can no longer say that it is prayer that continues. It is actually His presence that continues with you. This is beyond prayer. Now a heavenly blessedness is yours. You begin to discover that God is more intimately present to you than you are to yourself, and a great awareness of the Lord begins to come to you.

I have said previously about each one of these experiences with the Lord, that the *only* way to find Him is by *turning within*. It is there, and there alone, you can find Him. Now you will discover that as soon as you close your eyes, you are enveloped in prayer. You will be amazed that He has blessed you so much.

It is at this point, therefore, that it is proper to introduce to you yet another experience; one that takes place deep within you.

There is born within you an internal conversation with God.

This conversation is highly enjoyable, and the most amazing thing about it is that no outward circumstances can interrupt it.

Now you see just how far that simple prayer you began with can lead you! The same thing can be said of the "prayer of simplicity" that was said of wisdom: "All good things come together in her." (Apocrypha)

And the same can be said of this deeper experience with the Lord. Godliness flows so sweetly and so easily from within the believer who has advanced this far that it even seems to be *his* very nature that pours itself out with such sweetness and ease. The spring of living water within the spirit breaks forth abundantly, producing every kind of goodness.

And what of sin? Sin seems so far removed from the believer at this point that he is hardly even aware of it.

When you have entered into this deeper realm of experience with Jesus Christ, what should be your response to circumstance, to outward events? Simply remain faithful in this state. Rest quietly before the Lord. Let this simple, quiet rest in Him always be your preparation for everything. You must keep this in mind: Your only purpose is to be filled to overflowing with the divine presence of Jesus Christ and, deep within you, to be prepared to receive from Him anything that He chooses to bestow upon you.

14

Silence

The point to which this venture has led us is a *state of silence* and *continuous prayer*.

Let us go back a little and take a closer look at this matter of silence. Why, for instance, is being silent before the Lord when you first come to Him so important? First of all, it is because your fallen nature is opposed to God's nature. The two are not at all alike. Secondly, Jesus Christ is the Word, the *speaking* Word. He *can* speak. He *can* be heard! But for the Word (Jesus Christ) to be received by you, *your* nature must be made to correspond to *His* nature.

Let me illustrate further.

Consider the act of hearing. Listening is a *passive* sense. If you ever want to hear anything, you must yeild a passive ear.

Jesus Christ is the Eternal Word. He, and He alone, is the source of new life to you. For you to have new life, He must be communicated to you. He can speak. He can communicate. He can impart new life. And when He desires to speak to you, He demands the most intense attention to His voice.

Now you can see why the Scripture so frequently urges you to listen, to be attentive to the voice of God.

Hearken unto Me, My people,
And give ear unto Me, Oh My nation.
(Isaiah 51:4)

Hear Me, all you whom I carry in
My bosom, and bear within My bowels.
(Isaiah 46:3)

Hearken, oh daughter, and consider and incline your ear; forget also your own people, and your father's house; so shall the king greatly desire your beauty.
(Psalm 45:10,11)

Here is how to begin to acquire this habit of silence. First of all, forget yourself. That is, lay aside all self-interest.

Secondly, listen attentively to God.

These two simple actions will gradually begin to produce in you a love of that beauty which *is* the Lord Jesus! This beauty is inwrought in you *by* Him.

One other thing. Try to find a quiet place. Outward silence develops inward silence; and outward silence improves inward silence as it begins to take root in your life.

It is impossible for you to really become inward, that is, to live in your inmost being where Christ lives, without loving silence and retirement.

Hosea said it well:

I will lead her into solitude,
And there I will speak to her heart.
(Hosea 2:14)

You are to be completely occupied, inwardly, with God. Of course, this is impossible if, at the same time, you are outwardly busied with a thousand trifles.

The Lord is *at* the center of your being; therefore, He must *become* the center of your being.

What are you to do when you become drawn away from this God who is your center? No matter what it is that draws you away, whether weakness or lack of faith, you must immediately turn within once more.

Be ready to turn within, again and again, no matter how often you are drawn away. Be ready to repeat this turning just as often as distractions occur.

It is not enough to be turned inwardly to your Lord an hour or two each day. There is little value in being turned within to the Lord unless the end result is an anointing and a spirit of prayer which continues with you during the whole day.

15

A New Look At Confession of Sin

Where does *confession* of sin and *examination* of your life concerning sin fit into the life of a Christian following this path? How does he deal with these important matters? Let us take this chapter to open up a clearer, *higher* view of self-examination and of confession of sin.

It is commonly taught that self-examination is something that should always precede confession of sin. Though this may be correct, the *manner* of self-examination is dictated by the level of your Christian experience.

I would recommend for a Christian whose spiritual state has actually advanced to the stage which was described in the preceding chapters that when you come to the Lord concerning sin and confession, you do this: *Lay your entire soul open before God.* You can be certain that the Lord will not fail to enlighten you concerning your sin. Your Lord *will* shine as a light in you; and through His shining, He will allow you to see the nature of all your faults.

You might say that when this brilliant light, which is Christ Himself, shines on you and in you, you are under examination. An examination is being given to you by

God when this happens. Since it is your Lord who is doing this, and no one else, you should simply remain peaceful and calm before Him as He carries out this exposing.

Depend upon your Lord, not on yourself, to expose your sin and to show you the extent of your sin.

Please understand this fact: It is not *your* diligence, it is not *your* examination of yourself that will enlighten you concerning your sin. Instead, it is God who does all the revealing.

You see, if you try to be the one who does the examining, there is a very good chance that you will *deceive* yourself. You will never *really* allow yourself to see your true state. That is the simple fact about the nature of your own self-love. "*We* call the evil *good*, and the good evil." (Isaiah 5:20)

Ah, not so when you come to your Lord. He can be so thorough, so exacting, and so demanding! There, before Him, you are in full exposure before the Sun of Righteousness. His divine beams make even your smallest faults visible. The proper way to deal with sin becomes so evident. You must abandon yourself into the hands of God, both in self-examination and in the confession of your sins.

A Christian does not begin his spiritual experience with the Lord on this level which I am describing. On the other hand, he can, through this "prayer of simplicity," eventually arrive at this level.

Once you have established such a relationship with your Lord, you will soon discover that no fault in you escapes the reproof of God. For instance, as soon as you commit a sin, you are immediately rebuked by an inward sense. It will be a kind of deep, inward burning. . . a tender confusion. You see, *all* things are exposed under the piercing glance of your Lord. He will not allow *any* sin to be hidden or concealed.

As for you, when the Lord has firmly established this relationship, you will have the sense that He has so completely found you out that each time His light focuses on the sin in your life, you have only one course. All you can do is turn very simply to Him and there bear all the pain and correction which He inflicts.

Continue in this experience with your Lord. After a period of time of experiencing Him in this way, the Lord will become more and more the *constant* examiner of your soul. It will not be *you* examining yourself, nor will it be seasonal. It will be the Lord, *constantly*.

If you remain faithful in giving yourself up to the Lord in this way, you will come to realize that the divine light of your Lord can really reveal your heart far more effectively than *all* your efforts ever could.

Let us go on a little farther now and consider *confession* of sin.

There is awaiting you a higher understanding and a higher experience of confession and repentance. Should you truly desire to walk these paths, you should be aware of something about confession of sin which is generally misunderstood.

In the past when you have confessed your sins to your Lord, you have most likely felt regret for those sins, have you not?

There is a *higher* experience of repentance, and there is a *deeper* experience of confession of sin than the feeling of regret. In fact, you will find those feelings of regret replaced by something else—replaced by a love and a tranquility. That love, that tranquility sweetly saturates your soul and, having saturated it thoroughly, takes full possession of it.

Repentance that is sweet? Confession of sin that brings love and tranquility? If you have never been instructed in such matters, you will naturally want to resist this love. You will, instead, have a human inclination to try to produce a sorrowful, contrite attitude before God.

It has often been told you that a sorrowful, contrite heart over your sins is a thing well-pleasing to God. This is true.

But consider this: Trying by your own effort to produce a contrite heart causes you to lose *genuine* repentance. What *is* genuine repentance? Have you ever had the experience of real, genuine repentance? Think back. Was it not a deep feeling of love pouring itself out within you?

It is that love, that deep sense of love within you, which is a much *purer* and much *higher* expression of repentance; higher than *anything* you could produce by your own effort. This love takes all other feelings of repentance, sums them up into one, and expresses the totality of repentance *much more* perfectly than if each part of repentance were individually expressed to the Lord.

When the Lord has established this relationship in your life, you will not need to trouble yourself to produce *your* feelings about your sin. God is working His expression of repentance into you in such a pure way.

God hates sin and to experience a repentance which is given to you wholly of God will bring you to hate sin as He hates it.

Dear reader, do not be anxious and do not be so eager for action. The purest love you can ever know is that love which comes to you when the Lord is working on your soul. So let *Him* work. You must just remain in the place He assigns to you. Agree with the instruction of a very wise man who said:

> Put your confidence in God; remain quiet where *He* has placed you.
>
> (Ecclesiastes 11:22)

As you walk on in the experience we have just described, you will notice something. You will be amazed at how *difficult* it is to *remember* your sins! Forget your sins? Is this proper? Yes! And such an experience should not cause you to be uneasy. *You see, forgetting your sins is a proof of your having been cleansed from them.*

It is a *good* thing to have forgotten your sins. It is best you forget *anything* that concerns you so that you can remember *only* God.

Keep in mind that what has been presented in this chapter is a *higher* experience of confession and a *deeper* experience of repentance; yet you can be absolutely certain that as you experience the Lord in this way, *He* does not allow your sins to be unexposed. On the other hand, if *you* do the exposing, *much* may be left undiscovered. That is *not* the case when it is the Lord who is examining you! Unlike you, He will bring all your faults to the light. Therefore, leave your examination to God. You will find your heart far more revealed than if you had tried to do it by your own efforts.

Dear reader, this must be made very clear: These instructions are not applicable to a Christian living on the level of experience in which the soul is still in the active state. These instructions are *not* for the soul that is still active. On that level of experience it is altogether right—and necessary—that the soul exert itself in dealing with sin.

The soul of a Christian exerts itself in proportion to where it is in spiritual advancement. The more the soul advances toward its center—that is, the farther it is removed from the surface—the *less* the soul exerts itself. (This is true in dealing with sin, in dealing with confession of sin, and in all other involvements of life as well.)

Should you come to this more advanced level, I exhort you, no matter what your circumstances, to begin all your comings to the Lord by a very simple, quiet waiting before Him.

In so doing, you allow *Him* to act freely within you. He can never be better received than by Himself.

16

The Scripture

For the last few chapters we have been discussing a deeper experience of Christ, and in the last chapter we looked at how to deal with sins and confession. Let us now go on to consider what other experiences with Christ await you as your experience with Him goes deeper still.

Let us take the Scripture first. Is there a deeper use you can make of the Scripture than has been mentioned up until now?

Remember, please, from an earlier chapter, that reading the Scripture is a way *into* prayer. Remember, too, that what you *read* may become *prayer*. Is there yet more the Scripture can provide? Yes, you can use the Scripture in yet a more refined manner than has been mentioned before. Let us consider that way. I will give you a brief, practical description.

First, come before the Lord and begin to read. Stop reading just as soon as you feel yourself being drawn inwardly. Stop reading when you feel the Lord drawing you in your inward parts to Himself. Now, simply remain in stillness. Stay there for a while. Then, momentarily, proceed with your reading; but read only a little. Always cease reading each time you feel a divine attraction drawing you deeper within.

What can you expect beyond this state?

From time to time you will *begin* to touch a *state of inward silence*. What shall be your response to such an experience? One thing is this: No longer burden yourself with spoken prayer. (At this time, to pray out loud, or in *any* conventional way, would only draw you away from an inward experience and draw you back to an outward, surface prayer.)

You will be *attracted* to silence so there is no reason to force yourself to speak.

But if you do not speak, *what* shall you do? Nothing! Simply yield to the inward drawing! Yield to the wooing of your spirit. Your spirit is drawing you deeper within.

One other word.

In all your experience of Christ, it is wisest for you to stay away from any set form, or pattern, or *way*. Instead, *be wholly given up to the leading of the Holy Spirit*.

By following your spirit, every encounter you have with the Lord is one that is *perfect*...no matter what the encounter is like.

17

Prayer Requests?

As you continue in this venture with Christ—this venture that began as a simple way of prayer—yet another experience may await you. It is this: Do not be too surprised if you find you are no longer able to offer up prayers of petition.

You may find that prayers of *request* become more difficult. Yes, it is true that in the past you offered up petitions and requests with complete ease. Until now, praying this way was never difficult. But in this new relationship with your Lord, it is the Spirit who prays! And as the Spirit prays, *He* helps your weakness. He is making intercession for you. And *He* is praying according to the will of God.

> For we do not know how to pray as we should; but the Spirit Himself intercedes for us with groanings too deep for words.
> (Romans 8:26)

There is your will; there is God's will. There is your plan; there is God's plan. There is your prayer; there is *His* prayer. You must agree to His plans. He takes from you all your own workings so that *His* may be substituted in their place.

Therefore, yield.

Let God do in you what He will.

In His prayers, which *He* prays, there is also His will. Let *Him* pray. Give up your own prayers; give up your own desires and your own requests. Yes, you have a will; yes, you have desires and requests. Nevertheless, let Him have the will, the desire, that is in the prayers *He* prays.

But this relationship goes even deeper.

In order for God to have that which is found in His prayer, then you, the one praying, must give up your attachment to everything. This means you must live a life *in which there is nothing you want!* Be attached to nothing, no matter how good it is or appears to be.

18

Distractions

Now that we have explored some of the encounters you will have in this venture—some of the things the Lord will introduce to you and some of the things He will demand from you—let us set this chapter aside for a practical matter. As you have read in previous chapters, there will be distractions, especially at the outset. And for quite some time afterward, your mind will be distracted from prayer. Let us take a brief look at this problem.

How do you deal with those things that distract; how do you handle those things that draw you away from the inmost part of your being? If you should sin (or even if it is only a matter of being distracted by some circumstances around you), what should you do?

You must instantly turn within to your spirit.

Once you have departed from God, you must return to Him as quickly as possible. There, once more with Him, receive any penalty He chooses to inflict.

But here is one thing you must be very careful about: Do *not* become distressed because your mind has wandered away. Always guard yourself from being anxious because of your faults. First of all, such distress only stirs up the soul and distracts you to outward things. Secondly, your distress really springs from a secret root of pride. What you are experiencing is, in fact, a love of your own worth.

To put it in other words, you are simply hurt and upset at seeing what you *really* are.

If the Lord should be so merciful as to give you a true spirit of His humility, you will not be surprised at your faults, your failures, or even your own basic nature.

The more clearly you see your true self, the clearer you also see how miserable your self nature really is; *and* the more you will abandon your whole being to God. Seeing that you have such a desperate need of Him, you will press toward a more intimate relationship with Him.

This is the way you should walk, just as the Lord Himself has said:

> I will instruct you and teach you in the way you shall go. I will guide you with My eyes.
> (Psalm 32:8)

19

Temptation

Temptations, as well as distractions, are a major problem you will encounter at the outset of your adventure into God. Be very careful in your attitude toward them. If you attempt to struggle directly with these temptations, you will only strengthen them; and in the process of this struggle, your soul will be drawn away from its intimate relationship with the Lord.

You see, a close, intimate relationship to Christ should *always* be your soul's only purpose. Therefore, when you are tempted toward sin or toward outward distractions—no matter the time, no matter the place, nor the provocation—*simply turn away* from that sin.

And as you turn, draw nearer to your Lord.

It is that simple.

What does a little child do when he sees something that frightens him or confuses him? He doesn't stand there and try to fight the thing. He will, in fact, hardly look at the thing that frightens him. Rather, the child will quickly run into the arms of his mother.

There, in those arms, he is safe.

In exactly the same way, you should turn from the dangers of temptation and *run* to your God!

God is in the midst of her, she shall not be moved; God shall help her, and that right early.

(Psalm 46:5)

You and I are very weak. At our best we are *very* weak. If you, in your weakness, attempt to attack your enemies, you will often find yourself wounded. Just as frequently, you will even find yourself defeated.

There is another way.

In times of temptation and distraction, remain by faith in the simple presence of Jesus Christ. You will find an immediate supply of strength.

This was David's resource and support:

I have set the Lord always before me.
Because He is at my right hand,
I shall not be moved.
Therefore, my heart is glad
And my glory rejoices;
My flesh also shall rest in hope.

(Psalm 16·8,9)

And again in Exodus, it says:

The *Lord* shall fight for you while you keep silent.

(Exodus 14:14)

20

Consumed

I would like to take this chapter to talk about a very important element in prayer, one that is almost totally overlooked.

If I were to say to you that one of the great elements of prayer is deep, inward worship, I am sure you would agree. We would both concur that without a deep, inward worship of the Lord we simply would not have *real* prayer. *Real* prayer, of necessity, has worship as its central element.

But there is another element to prayer, just as central, just as essential, as worship. And it is right here that we come to the central issue of man with God; moreover, without this element there is no real prayer; without it there can be no plunging into the very depths of Jesus Christ. Without this element there is no real prayer, no entrance into the depths of Christ, and no way that God can bring you to the ends which He plans for you.

And what is this aspect of prayer?

The *giving up of self* is a necessary part of prayer and of experiencing the depths of Jesus Christ.

(So once more we have stepped beyond prayer. Real prayer demands of the one praying that he utterly abandon self. Moreover, God desires that such a state ultimately become yours at *all* times.)

It is the Apostle John who speaks of *prayer* as being an incense—an incense whose smoke ascends to God and is received by Him.

> Unto the angel was given much incense, that he should offer it with the prayers of all the saints.
>
> (Revelation 8:3)

As you come to the Lord, pour out your heart in the presence of God. Prayer *is* the outpouring of your heart to Him. "I have poured out my soul before the Lord," said Hannah, the mother of Samuel. (I Samuel 1:15) This outpouring is an incense, and this incense is a total giving of your self to Him.

The incense offered by the wise men, laid at the feet of Christ in the stable of Bethlehem, is a picture of outpoured prayer to Him.

What is prayer? Prayer is a certain warmth of love. Ah, but more! Prayer is a melting! Prayer is a dissolving and an uplifting of the soul. This warmth of love, this melting, this dissolving and uplifting causes the soul to ascend to God.

As the soul is melted, sweet fragrances begin to rise from it. These fragrances pour forth from a consuming fire of love. . .and that love is in you. It is a consuming fire of love in your inmost being, a fire of love for God.

An illustration of this incense, this love, and this pouring forth is found in the Song of Songs. The young maiden says, "While the King was at His table, my perfume gave forth its fragrance." (Song of Songs 1:12) Let us look at that scene more closely.

First, let us look at the table.

The table referred to here is the inmost part of your being, your spirit. And there *in* your spirit God dwells. Oh, when you have learned how to dwell there with Him, His divine presence dissolves the hardness of your soul. And as that hardness of your soul melts, precious fragrances pour forth from it!

Now look at the King. Look at "the Beloved." Upon seeing the Bride's soul melt, He speaks:

> Who is this!...coming up from the wilderness like columns of smoke, perfumed with myrrh and frankincense?
>
> (Song of Solomon 3:6)

Now we must ask the central question: *How* does the soul ascend to God?

The soul ascends to God by giving up *self*, giving it up to the destroying power of divine love! Yes, giving up to the annihilating power of divine love!

This giving up of self is essential, absolutely essential, if you are to plumb, experience, and continually dwell in the depths of Jesus Christ. It is only by the destruction and annihilation of self that you can pay homage to the sovereignty of God!

You see,

> The power of the Lord is great, and He is honored only by the humble.
>
> (Apocrypha)

Let us see if we can understand this just a little more clearly.

It is by the utter destruction of self that you acknowledge the supreme existence of God.

The hour must come when *you* cease *all* living in the realm of the self! You must *cease to exist in self* so that the Spirit of the Eternal Word may exist in you.

By the giving up of your own life, you make way for His coming! And it is in your dying that *He* lives!

Can this be made practical? Yes!

You must surrender your whole being to Jesus Christ, ceasing to live any longer in yourself, so that He may become your life.

> For you *have* died, and your life is hidden with Christ in God.
>
> (Colossians 3:3)

> Pass into Me all you who earnestly seek after Me.
>
> (Apocrypha)

But how do you pass into God? By *forsaking* your self that you may be lost in Him!

You can be lost in Him *only* by the annihilation of the self. And what has that to do with prayer? The annihilation of self *is* the true prayer of worship! It is a prayer you must learn—learn in all the totality of its deepest possible meaning. *This* is the experience that renders to God, and to God alone, all "blessing, honor, glory, and power, forever and ever." (Revelation 5:13)

This experience, this prayer, is the *prayer of reality*. This is *reality!* Annihilation is worshipping God in spirit and in reality. (John 4:23)

All true worship is "in spirit." To be "in spirit," the soul is annihilated. "In spirit" you enter into the purity of that Spirit that prays within you; you are drawn away from your own soulish and human methods of prayer. You are "in reality" because you are placed in the reality of the *all* of God and the *nothing* of man.

Dear reader, there are, in fact, only two truths: the All and the Nothing.

Everything else is a lie. God is All; you are nothing. The only way you can pay due honor to God is by your own annihilation. As soon as this wonderful work is done, God moves in.

There is a principle of nature here: The Lord never allows a void or an emptiness in nature to remain. He comes to the place of nothingness—of emptiness— and instantly fills it with Himself.

He puts Himself in the very place of that which He has put to death!

But is not annihilation a bitter thing? Oh! If only you knew the virtue and the blessing which the soul receives from having passed into this experience. Taste it and you will be willing to have nothing else. *This* is the "pearl of great price," "the hidden treasure." Whoever finds it, freely sells all that he has in order to purchase it. (Matthew 13:44,45)

This is the "well of living water, which springs up to everlasting life." (John 4:14)

Do you recall that the Lord Jesus told us that "the kingdom of God is within us"? (Luke 17:21) This is true in two ways.

It is true first when God becomes the Master and Lord

within you so completely that *nothing* in you resists His dominion. It is then that your inner being, your spirit, *is* His kingdom. That is when God *possesses* you.

Secondly, there is the matter of your possessing God. When we possess God, we also possess His kingdom; and in His kingdom there is fulness of joy. Our ultimate purpose is to enjoy God. . .*in this life.* To enjoy God! *This* is the very purpose for which we were created.

Alas, so few realize that this is attainable and so easily laid hold of.

To serve God is to reign!

21

Silence—in the Depths

Let us go on now to the part silence plays in our advancing experience of Christ, for silence has a great deal to do with experiencing the Lord on a deeper plane.

On occasion some people have heard the term "the prayer of silence" and have concluded that the role the soul is to play in this prayer is one of dullness, deadness and inactivity. This, of course, is not the case. As a matter of fact, the soul plays a higher, more extensive role than in spoken prayer.

How is this possible?

The soul can be active and yet utterly silent. This is because it is the Lord Himself who has become the mover of the soul. The soul acts in response to the moving of *His* Spirit.

> For all who are being led by the Spirit, these are the sons of God.
>
> (Romans 8:14)

Therefore, to engage in "the prayer of silence" does not mean that you cease all action. Instead, it means your soul acts by the moving of your spirit.

Perhaps Ezekiel can help us see this. Ezekiel had a vision of wheels. These wheels he saw had the living

Spirit with them. Wherever the Spirit went, there the wheels went. If the Spirit stood still, the wheels stood still. If the Spirit ascended up from the earth into the heavens, the wheels rose up close beside.

The Spirit was in those wheels, and the wheels were moved by the Spirit. (Ezekiel 1:19-21) The soul is like those wheels. The soul can be active after its own things, or it can wait—wait until something deeper stirs. Then the soul becomes like those wheels, following the Spirit wherever it goes. The soul should, in the same way, yield to the leading of the living Spirit within. The soul should wait and be faithful to act *only* when the Spirit moves.

You can be sure that the Spirit *never* exalts the self-nature. (The soul, following its own inclination, so often does exalt the self.) What does the Spirit do? The Spirit moves forward, plunging toward the *ultimate* end. And what is that ultimate end? It is union with God.

Therefore, let the soul do nothing of itself in prayer. The soul must simply follow the Spirit until it reaches its ultimate end!

By this illustration I believe you can see that the soul does not cease all action. Its action is simply in perfect concert with the Spirit.

Let us go on now to consider "the prayer of silence" in a practical way. How do you begin to experience the Lord in an attitude of silence?

You see, when your soul is active on its own—that is, active *apart* from the activity of the Spirit—then by its very nature its activity is forced and strained! The soul's effort in prayer is *always* that of anxiety and striving.

This is actually to your advantage! You can easily distinguish when the soul is functioning!

Oh! All is so different when the soul is responding to the moving of the Spirit—responding to something far deeper within your being.

When the soul is responding to the Spirit, the action is free, easy and natural. It will seem that you are putting forth almost no effort at all.

> He brought me forth
> into a large place;
> He delivered me,
> because He delights in me.
>
> (Psalm 18:19)

Once your soul has turned within and once your mind is set on the Spirit, from that moment on the inward attraction of the Lord's Spirit is very powerful. In fact, the attraction of your spirit toward the soul is stronger than any other force—stronger than those things which would draw you back to the surface.

The truth is, nothing is as quick to return to its center as is the soul to the Spirit!

Is the soul active at this time? Yes! But the activity is so exalted, so natural, so peaceful, and so spontaneous that it will seem to you that your soul is making no effort at all!

Have you ever noticed that when a wheel rolls slowly, it is easy to see all of it. But as the wheel turns faster, you can distinguish very little. *This* is the soul at rest in God. When the soul is at rest in God, its activity is spiritual and very exalted. Nonetheless, the soul is engaging in *no* effort. It is full of peace.

Therefore, hold your soul at peace.

The more peaceful your soul is, the more quickly it is able to move toward God, its center.

How is this possible? Because the soul is yielded to the spirit, and it is the Spirit that is moving and directing!

What is attracting you so strongly to your inward parts? It is none other than God Himself. And, oh, *His* drawing of you causes you to run to Him.

The girl in the Song of Songs understood this, for she said:

> Draw me,
> We will run after You.
> (Song of Solomon 1:4)

"Draw me to Yourself, Oh my Divine Center, by the secret springs of my existence, and all my powers and senses will follow you!"

The Lord is so simple in His attraction of you. This attraction of His is both an ointment to heal and a perfume to allure you to Himself. The maiden in the Song of Songs said it:

> We follow the fragrance of Your perfume!
> (Song of Solomon 1:3)

"Lord, You attract us by the *fragrance* of Your very being, and You draw us so deeply within to Yourself!"

His attracting force is extremely powerful, and yet the soul follows freely and without force. Why? Because the attracting of your Lord is just as delightful as it is powerful! Although His attracting of you is powerful, it carries you away by its sweetness.

When the young maiden said, "Draw me, and we will run after you," she was speaking, first of all, of her spirit—the center of her being. It is the spirit which is being drawn. The Lord speaks to your spirit; He calls you to follow Him by drawing your center where there is only Himself. So your spirit is attracted first. You, in turn, follow the attraction of the center. You do so by turning your attention and all the powers of your soul on Him. "Draw *me*"—see the oneness of your center, your spirit, as it is drawn to Him who is the very inmost part of your center. "*We* will run after you"—see how the senses and powers of the soul follow the attraction of the center.

We are not promoting the idea that the soul should be lazy or inactive. We are encouraging the highest activity the soul can engage in: total dependence on the Spirit of God. This should always be your main concern. It is "in Him alone that we live and move and have our being." (Acts 17:28)

This simple, humble dependence on the Spirit of God is necessary above all other things. This constant dependence on our part will soon cause the soul to reach that unity and that simplicity for which it was created.

We are so complex; our souls are capable of so much diverse activity. We must leave these ways so that we will be free—free to enter the simplicity and the unity of God. Oh, to return into God, into the One in whose image we were originally formed! (Genesis 1:27)

Your Lord is simple; He is one. But when you enter into the unity of God, His oneness does not rule out the great variety that is the expression of His nature. Just as we enter into His unity when we are united to His Spirit and are made one with Him, in the same way we are also able to carry out the various aspects of His will when we are united with Him. And we can do this without having to leave that state of union with God. The variety of His will *can* be carried out without the sacrifice of our oneness with Him.

So now you perhaps can see where the simple "prayer of silence" can lead!

Let us go on!*

Yield yourself to the guidance of the Spirit of God. By continuing to depend upon His action, and not that action of the soul, the things you do will be of value to God. Only what you do in *this* way is of value to God and to His work on this earth.

Let us see this from God's point of view.

> All things were made by the Word,
> and without Him was not anything
> made that was made.
>
> (John 1:3)

In the very beginning it was God who formed man by His Word. He made man in His own image. God was Spirit and He gave man a spirit so that He could come into him and mingle His own life with man's life.

This, of course, was the state of man before the Fall. At the time of the Fall, man's spirit was deadened. God lost

---

*As the soul is drawn into this relationship, something new is discovered. It is this: The Spirit, like the soul, is also very active! The Spirit is full of activity. Yet it is not the same activity as the soul. When *you* have been moved by the Lord, your activity will be much more energetic than if it were the activity of your own self nature. That Spirit is more active than *any* other force.

His chance to move into man's spirit. Man lost the ability to contain the life of God and to bear the image of God.

It was very plain to see that if God were ever to restore man to what He intended him to be, man's spirit would *have* to be restored.

And how could God restore man's spirit? How could He restore the image of God in man?

By none less than Jesus Christ. It had to be the Lord Jesus Himself who gave life to man's spirit and restored the image of God. Why? Because Jesus Christ alone is the exact image of His Father. He alone brings the life of God into man.

No image can be repaired by its own efforts. The broken image has to remain passive under the hand of the workman.

What is your activity in this restoration? Your only activity should be to yield yourself completely to the inner workings of the Spirit. Jesus Christ has come into you, into your inmost parts. Yield to His workings there.

If a canvas is unsteady, the artist is unable to paint an accurate picture upon it. The same is true of you. Every movement of the self produces error. The activity of the self interrupts and defeats the design which Jesus Christ wishes to engrave upon you. You must, instead, simply remain at peace. Respond *only* to the Spirit's working.

Jesus Christ has life in Himself (John 5:26), and *He* must give life to every living thing.

This principle—the principle of utter dependence upon the Spirit and complete denial of the activity of the soul—can be seen in the church.

Look at the church. The Spirit of the church is a

moving, life-giving Spirit. Is the church idle and barren and unfruitful? No! The church is *full* of activity. But her activity is this: complete dependence on God's Spirit. That Spirit moves her. That Spirit gives her life.

This principle functions in the church, and it is this principle which causes the church to be what she is. The exact same principle should operate in you! What is true of her should be true of her members. To be her spiritual children, you must be led by the Spirit.

The Spirit in you *is* active. The activity that is produced in your life as a result of following the Spirit is a much higher activity than any other.

(An activity is worthy of only as much praise as its source. An activity that comes as a result of following the Spirit is more praise-worthy than any other activity coming from any other source. Whatever is produced from God's Spirit is divine. Whatever comes from self, no matter how good it appears, is still only human, still only the self.)

Your Lord once declared that He alone has life. All other creatures have "borrowed" life. The Lord has life *in* Himself. That life, which is *in Him,* also carries with it *His* nature. This is the unique life which He desires to give to you. He wishes to give you divine life, and He wishes you to live by that life instead of the life of your soul. At the same time, you should make room for denying your soul, that is, denying the activity of your own life. The only way you can make room for the life of God to dwell in you and to live in you is by losing your old Adam life and denying the activity of the self.

Why? Because this life you are receiving is the very life of God, the same life God lives by! Paul said,

If any man be in Christ
he is a new creature;
old things are passed away;
behold, all things have become new!
(II Corinthians 5:17)

But, and I repeat, the only way this becomes practical experience to you is by dying to yourself and to all your own activity so that the activity of God can be substituted in its place.

Going back, then, to what was said at the beginning of the chapter, the "prayer of silence" does not forbid activity; it encourages it. It encourages the divine activity of your spirit; it discourages the lower activity of your soul. Such a prayer, then, must be in absolute dependence on the Spirit of God. The activity of the Spirit must *take the place* of your own. Such an exchange can only take place with man's consent.

In giving your consent, you must also, of course, begin to cease your own activity. The outcome will be that, little by little, the activity of God can completely take the place of the activity of the soul.

There is a beautiful example of this in the Gospels. You will recall that Martha was doing something which was very correct, and yet the Lord rebuked her! Why? Because what she was doing, she was doing in her own strength. Martha was not following the moving of the Spirit within her.

You must realize, dear reader, that the soul of man is naturally restless and turbulent. Your soul accomplishes very little even though it always appears busy.

The Lord said to Martha, "You are careful and

troubled over so many things. But only one thing is needed! Mary has chosen that good part which shall not be taken from her." (Luke 10:41-42)

And what had Mary chosen? She had chosen to rest peacefully and tranquilly at the feet of Jesus. She had ceased to live that Christ might be her life!

This illustration highlights just how necessary it is for you to deny yourself and all your activity to follow Jesus Christ. *If you are not led by His Spirit, you cannot follow Him.*

When His life comes in, your life must be put away. Paul said, "He that is joined to the Lord is one Spirit. (I Corinthians 6:17)

David once said how good it was to draw near to the Lord and to put his trust in Him. (Psalm 73:28) What does it mean to "draw near to God"?

Drawing near to God is, in fact, *the beginning of union!*

We began this chapter speaking of the prayer of silence. We then went on to the soul's following the Spirit in perfect concert. Now we have come to the final, deepest experience with God—the ultimate Christian experience. It is union with God.

The experience of union with God comes to us in four stages: its *beginning*, its *progress*, its *achievement*, and its *consummation*. (We will discuss the experience of union in the final chapter of this book.)

The experience of union begins very simply when there is born in you a desire for God. And when is that? When the soul begins to turn inward to the life of the Spirit; when the soul begins to fall under the powerful, magnetic attraction of that Spirit. *At this point*, an earnest desire for union with God is *born*!

Once your soul has begun to turn within to the Spirit, it moves nearer and nearer to God. This is the *progress* toward union.

Finally, the soul is *one* spirit with Him. It is here at last that the soul, which has wandered so far away from God, returns again to the place for which it was created!

You must enter into this realm. Why? Because *this* is the purpose of *all* God's working in you.

> If any man does not have the Spirit of Jesus Christ, he does not belong to Him.
> (Romans 8:9)

For you to be utterly Christ's you must be filled with His Spirit and emptied of your own self-life. Paul tells us just how necessary it is to be of this Spirit.

> As many as are led by the Spirit of God, these are the sons of God.
> (Romans 8:14)

There is a Spirit! And the Spirit who makes us sons of God is the same Spirit who does the working of God deep within us.

> You have not received the Spirit of bondage again to fear; but you have received the Spirit of adoption whereby you cry "Abba, Father."
> (Romans 8:15)

Who is this Spirit that works in you? He is none other

than the Spirit of Jesus Christ. Through this Spirit we are made to share in His Sonship.

> The Spirit bears witness with our spirit that we are children of God.
>
> (Romans 8:16)

When you yield yourself to the leading of this wonderful One, you will sense within you that you are a son of God. Furthermore, you will know the added joy of receiving, "not the spirit of slavery, but of liberty, even the liberty of the children of God." (Romans 8:15) Expect this to be the outcome of your walk. You will discover that you are able to act freely and easily, and yet you will also act with strength and certainty.

The working of the Spirit deep within you must be the *source* of all your activity. Let me repeat: All activity—both that which is surface and visible, as well as that which is hidden and internal—must come from the working of the Spirit.

Paul illustrates this in the book of Romans. He shows us our ignorance even in what we pray for. He declares that it is the Spirit who *must* pray.

> The Spirit also helps our weakness, for we do not know how to pray as we should; but the Spirit Himself intercedes for us with groanings too deep for words.
>
> (Romans 8:26)

This is plain enough: *We do not know what we need!* We do not know how to pray for the things we need. In fact, *we* do not know *how* to pray! Ah, but the Spirit who lives inside us knows what and how to pray. The One to whom you have given yourself knows everything!

If that be true, shouldn't you therefore allow Him to pour out His unutterable groanings on your behalf?

You cannot always be sure about your own prayer. But, oh, the Spirit is *always* heard when He prays.

The Lord Jesus said to His Father, "I know that you *always* hear me." (John 11:42) It follows that if you freely allow the Spirit to pray and to intercede in place of your own prayers, then the prayers He prays from within you will be heard—always!

Is this a certainty?

Listen to the words of Paul, that skillful mystic and master of the inward life.

> He who searches the heart knows what the mind of the Spirit is because He intercedes for the saints according to the will of God.
> (Romans 8:27)

The Spirit seeks only what is the will of God! At last, here is One who is wholly abandoned to the will of God! The Spirit utters in prayer *only* what is the will of God.

God's will is that you be saved; His will is that you be perfect. Therefore, the Spirit is interceding in you for all that is necessary for your perfection.

If the Spirit is fully able to care for all your need, why should you burden yourself with unnecessary cares? Why weary yourself with so much activity, never stopping to enter the rest of God?

Tne Lord invites you to cast all your care on Him.

The Lord—who is full of mercy—once complained that the soul wastes its strength and its treasures on a thousand outward things. Yet all the desires of the soul can easily be satisfied.

> Why do you spend money for what is not bread, and your wages for what does not satisfy? Listen carefully to me, and eat that which is good, and delight yourself in abundance.
>
> (Isaiah 55:2)

Come to know the joy of listening to God in this way, dear reader! How greatly your soul is strengthened by so *hearing* your Lord.

> Be silent, all flesh, before the Lord.
>
> (Zechariah 2:13)

All things must cease when *He* appears.

The Lord is calling you to an even greater abandonment...one with *nothing* held back. He has assured you that there is nothing to fear because He takes very special care of you.

> Can a woman forget her nursing child and have no compassion on the son of her womb? Even these may forget, *but I will not forget you.*
>
> (Isaiah 49:15)

How much comfort there is in these words! Who, after hearing this, will fear abandoning himself wholly to the call of God?

22

The Constant State

We will begin this chapter with this simple point: Your spiritual experiences fall into two categories—those that are external (surface) and those that take place internally, deep within your being. There are activities or actions that you form: some are surface; some are deeper.

Your external activities are those which can be seen outwardly. They have to do with, more or less, physical things. Now this you must see: There is no real goodness in them, no spiritual growth in them, and very *little* experience of Christ!

Of course, there is an exception: If your outward actions are a result (a by-product) of something that has taken place deep within you, then these outward actions *do* receive spiritual value and they *do* possess real goodness. But outward activities have only as much spiritual value as they receive from their source.

Our way, therefore, is clear. We must give our full attention to those activities that take place deep within our inmost being. *These* are the activities of the Spirit. The Spirit is inward, not outward. You turn inward to your spirit and, in so doing, turn away from outward activities and outward distractions.

Inward activity begins by simply turning within to Jesus Christ, for that is where He is, within your spirit.

You should continually be turning within to God.

Give Him all your attention; pour out all the strength of your being purely on Him.

> Reunite all the motions of your heart in the holiness of God.
>
> (Apocrypha)

David expressed it so well when he said, "I will keep my whole strength for You." (Psalm 59:9)

How is this done? By earnestly turning to God, who is always there within you.

Isaiah said, "Return to your heart." (Isaiah 46:8) Each of us, by sinning, has turned from our heart, and it is *only* the heart that God desires.

> My son, give me your heart and let your eyes delight in my ways.
>
> (Proverbs 23:26)

What does it mean to give your whole heart to God? To give your whole heart to God is to have all the energy of your soul always centered on Him.

It is in this way we are conformed to His will.

If you are new in this voyage, your spirit is not yet strong. Your soul is easily turned to outward, physical things; it is very easy for you to become distracted from the Lord, your Center.

How far you turn away from Him will depend on how much you yield to the distractions and how far you allow yourself to be drawn away to surface things. In like manner, the means you use to return to God will depend on how far you have turned from Him. If you have only turned slightly, only the slightest turning again will be necessary.

As soon as you notice yourself straying from the Lord, you should *deliberately* turn your attention within to the living God. Re-enter your spirit; return at once to that place where you really belong: in Him. The more complete that turning is, the more complete will be your return to the Lord.

Rest assured that you will remain there—in God—just as long as your attention is centered upon the Lord Jesus Christ. What will hold you there? You will be held there by the powerful influence of that simple, unpretentious turning of your heart to God.

Repeat this simple turning within to the Lord again and again, as often as you are distracted. Be assured that eventually this turning will become your consistent experience.

But what will you do until then?

Until then simply keep *returning* to Him each time you have wandered away. When something is repeated over and over, it becomes a *habit*. This is true even of your soul. After much practice your soul forms the *habit* of turning inward to God.

In other words, the more you progress in Christ, the more you will continually abide with Him, without repeatedly straying and having to return. Your turning will become less and less outward. Eventually the turning will become imperceptible as a surface, or conscious, action and will take place deep within you.

What began as something quite sporadic—something that was a conscious, deliberate action—becomes habitual and continuous, without interruption. A continuous, inner act of abiding begins to take place within you.*

What do I mean by this continuous inner abiding?

To be *continuously* turned deep inside simply means that, having turned within to God—by a direct act—you have *remained* in His presence. You have no further need to keep turning to Christ; you already abide with Him in the chambers of your spirit. The only time you need to make a point of turning again is when your abiding is interrupted for some reason.

At this point in your spiritual life, you should not concern yourself with *trying* to turn to the Lord by any outward means. You will even find it difficult to make a deliberate, outward act of turning when you have begun this inner abiding.

You see, you are already turned within to the Lord; any outward activity will only draw you away from your union with Him.

To form the act of turning within, *that* is the goal! When this act has been formed in you, it will express itself as a continual abiding in your spirit and a continuous exchange of love between you and the Lord. Once this goal is attained, there is no longer any need to seek after it by *outward* acts. You may forget the outward act of trying to love the Lord and to be loved

*For some Christians, this abiding with God comes slowly, by degrees. Progress is gauged only as it is seen over an extended period of time. For other Christians, there is a continuous abiding from the very beginning. It does not matter which lot God has decreed for you. Simply keep turning within to God.

by Him. Instead, just continue on as you are. You should simply remain near to God *by* this continuous inner abiding.

In this state of continually being turned to God, you are abiding in the love of God, and the man who abides in love abides in God. (I John 4:16) You rest. But what does that mean? You *rest* in the *continuously* inward act of abiding.

Now, in this state of rest, is your soul active or passive? It is active! You are not in a passive state, even if you are resting. But what activity could there be in resting? You are resting in the act of abiding in His love. Can that be activity? Yes! Inside your spirit there is an act going on. It is *a sweet sinking into Deity.*

The inward attraction—the magnetic pull— becomes more and more powerful. Your soul, dwelling in love, is drawn by this powerful attraction and sinks continually deeper into that love.

So you see, this inward activity has become far greater than it was when your soul first began to turn inward. Under the powerful attraction of God drawing you into Himself, the inward activity has increased!

The difference is that at the outset the activity was more outward; now the activity has moved inside; it has become deep, inward, hidden and outwardly imperceptible.

To that Christian who is totally given up to God (that is, a Christian in whom *this* activity is taking place continually), there is *not even an awareness of all these things!* He cannot sense this activity because it is all a direct, inward turning to God. *Nothing* is outward or surface.

This is the reason some Christians who have touched upon this state have reported that they do *nothing*, that there is no activity and no turning taking place within them.

Unwittingly, they are mistaken about their own internal state; they are, in fact, more active than ever before and are continually turning to God. (They *act* each time they turn inward and return to God.)

The better report would be to say they do not *sense* any distinct activity, *not* that they have no activity within.

Oh, it is true that they are not *acting* (or turning) *of themselves*. However, they *are* being drawn, and they are *following* the attraction. *Love* is the weight which sinks them.

If you were to fall into the sea, and were that sea infinite, you would fall from one depth to another for all eternity. This is how it is with a Christian who is in that place of continuous abiding. He is not even aware of his descent, and yet he is sinking with inconceivable swiftness to the most inward depths of God.

We are now at a point where we can draw some conclusions concerning the subject of this chapter.

First, let us not say we do not form the act of turning to God. We do. Each of us does turn within. The way we do it, that is a different matter. The way we turn within is not the same for everyone.

Here is the error, though, of the new Christian. Every person who desires to turn to God to abide with Him just naturally expects to *feel* the Lord's presence and to experience Him *outwardly*.

This just cannot always be.

The outward experience is for the *beginner!* There are *other* experiences; these experiences are *much* deeper and far more inward. Such deeper experiences are laid hold of by those Christians who have progressed somewhat in spiritual experience.

Is the outward feeling of the Lord's presence to be disdained? Most certainly not! It is true that the outward acts are very weak touches with the Lord; and furthermore, they are of little value. For you to stop there is to deprive yourself of the deeper experiences of a more mature Christian. But—and you should be very clear about this—it is a great error for a new Christian—for you—to attempt a deep, inner walk without *first* experiencing the outward turning to Christ and *knowing* that *outward* sense of His presence.

The writer of Ecclesiastes said it: "To everything there is a season." (Ecclesiastes 3:1) This is especially true of your soul. Every state of transformation the soul passes through has a beginning, a progress, and a consummation. To stop at the beginning of any one of these stages is foolish. You must go through a period of learning, then a period of progress. At first you toil diligently, but at last you reap the fruit of your labor!

Let me illustrate. When sailors first take a ship out of port, it is very difficult to head her out to sea. They must use all their strength to get that ship clear of the harbor. But once she is at sea she moves easily in whatever direction the seamen choose.

It is the same with you as you begin to turn within to God. You are like that ship. At first you are very strongly bound by sin and by self. *Only* through a great deal of repeated effort are you turned within. But eventually those ropes which bind you have to loosen!

Keep on turning within!

Do so despite every failure! Despite all the distractions that pull you away!

If you will remain faithful and strong in this continual turning, gradually you will push off from the port of self. Leaving it far behind, you will head for the *interior* to an inner abiding with God, for *that* is your destination!

What happens once the ship has left port? She moves farther and farther out into the deep sea, and the farther from port she goes, the easier she moves.

There comes a time, at last, when she can use her sails! Her oars are useless. They are laid aside! Now her course is swift!

And what does the pilot do? He is content to spread the sails and hold the rudder. All he does now is keep the swiftly moving vessel *gently* on its course.

"To spread the sails" is to lay yourself before God in simple prayer. "To spread the sails" is to be moved by His Spirit.

"To hold the rudder" is to keep your heart from wandering away from its true course. "To hold the rudder" is to recall the heart, gently. You guide it firmly by the moving of the Spirit of God.

Now, as you begin to move into Him, He will gradually gain possession of your heart. He gains it in the same way—little by little—that the gentle breeze fills the sails and moves the ship forward.

When the winds are favorable, the pilot rests from his work. The pilot rests and leaves the ship to be moved by the wind. Oh, what progress they make without becoming the least bit tired!

They are making more progress in one hour without any effort than they ever did before even when exerting all their strength. If the oars were used now, it would only slow the ship and cause fatigue. The oars are useless and unnecessary.

You have just seen a description of your proper *inward* course.

If *God* is your mover, you will go much farther in a short time than all your repeated self-effort could *ever* do.

Dear reader, try this path! You will eventually find it to be the easiest in the world.

23

To Christian Workers

As we draw near the close of this little book, I would like to address a word of exhortation to those Christian workers who are in charge of new converts.

Let us consider the present situation. All around us, Christians are seeking to convert the lost to Jesus Christ. What is the best way to do this? And once men have been converted, what is the best way to aid them in attaining full perfection in Christ?

The way to reach the lost is to reach them by the *heart*. If a new convert were introduced to *real prayer* and to a *true inward experience of Christ* as soon as he became converted, you would see countless numbers of converts go on to become true disciples.

On the other hand, you can see that the present way of dealing only with external matters in the life of the new convert brings little fruit. Burdening the new Christian with countless rules and all sorts of standards does not help him grow in Christ. Here is what should be done: The new Christian should be led to God.

How?

By learning to turn within to Jesus Christ *and* by giving the Lord his whole heart.

If you are one of those in charge of new believers, lead them to a *real inner knowledge* of Jesus Christ. Oh, what a difference there would be in the lives of those new Christians!

Consider the results!

We would see the simple farmer, as he plowed his field, spend his days in the blessing of the presence of God. The shepherd, while watching his flocks, would have the same abandoned love for the Lord which marked the early Christians. The factory worker, while laboring with his outward man, would be renewed with strength in his inner man.

You would see each of these people put away every kind of sin from his life; all would become spiritual men and women with hearts set on knowing and experiencing Jesus Christ.

For a new Christian—for all of us in fact—the heart is all important if we are to go forward in Christ. Once the heart has been gained by God, everything else will eventually take care of itself. This is why He requires the heart above all else.

Dear reader, it is by the Lord gaining your heart, and no other way, that all your sins can be put away. If the heart could be gained, Jesus Christ would reign in peace, and the whole church would be renewed.

In fact, we are discussing the very thing that caused the early church to lose its life and beauty. It was the loss of a deep, inner, spiritual relationship to Christ. Counterwise, the church could soon be *restored* if this inner relationship were recovered!

That is not all. Right now Christian leaders are quite preoccupied with the fear that the Lord's people will fall into some doctrinal error. Oh, but when Christians are believing in Jesus Christ and drawing near to Him, there is little danger of such a thing ever happening!

You can be sure that if a Christian turns away from the Lord, he can discuss doctrine and engage in arguments all day long, but none of it will help him! Endless discussion only brings *more* confusion. What that believer needs is for someone to direct him to simply believe in Jesus Christ and to turn within to Him. Were any believer to do so, he would very soon be led back to God!

What inexpressible damage new Christians—for that matter, *most* Christians—have suffered because of the loss of an inner, spiritual relationship to Jesus Christ.

You who are in authority over young believers must yourself one day give an account to God for those who have been entrusted to you by the Lord. You will have to give an account for not having discovered for yourself this hidden treasure—this inner relationship to Christ—and you will also be held accountable for not having *given* that treasure to those in your charge.

Nor will you, in that day, be able to excuse yourself by saying that this walk with the Lord was too dangerous or that simple, uneducated people are unable to understand spiritual things. The Scripture simply does not validate these conjectures.

What about the dangers of walking in this way? Are there any?

What danger can there be in walking in the only true way: *in* Jesus Christ? What danger is there in giving yourself up completely to the Lord Jesus and fixing all your attention continually on Him? Can any harm come from placing all your confidence in His grace and in loving Him purely with all the love and passion your heart is capable of pouring out?

As for the simple and the unlearned, it is *not* true they are incapable of this inner relationship to Christ. The reverse is true. They are actually more suited to it.

The Lord loves those who walk simply. (Proverbs 12:22)

Their humility, their simple trust in God, and their obedience make it easier for them to turn within and follow the Lord's Spirit. They are more qualified than most! You see, these simple believers are not accustomed to analyzing; they do not have the habit of discussing the issues of everything; and they are quick to let go of their own opinions.

Yes, they do lack a great deal of education and religious training; *therefore*, they are freer and quicker to follow the leading of the Spirit. Other people—more gifted, better educated, trained in theology—are often cramped and even blinded by their spiritual wealth! Such a person very often offers greater resistance to the inner anointing and to the leading of the Lord's Spirit.

The Psalmist tells us,

> Unto the simple God gives the understanding of *His* law.
> (Psalm 119:130)

Furthermore, we have been assured that God loves to give Himself to those who need Him.

> The Lord cares for the simple. I was reduced to extremity and He saved me.
> (Psalm 116:6)

If you are one who has new believers in your care, be careful of preventing these children from coming to Jesus Christ. Remember that He said to His first disciples: "Let the children alone and do not hinder them from coming to Me; the kingdom of the heavenlies belongs to such as these." (Matthew 19:14) (It was the disciples' attempt to prevent the children from coming to Jesus Christ that caused Him to make this statement.)

It has been the habit of man throughout the ages to heal people by applying some remedy to the outward body when, in fact, the disease is deep inside. Why do converts remain basically unchanged despite so much effort? It is because those over them have dealt only with the *outward* matters of their lives. There is a better way: Go straight to the heart!

Laying down rules and trying to change the outward behavior will *not* produce a work that will endure in the life of a Christian.

Then what is the answer? *Give the new convert the key to his spirit,* to the inward parts of his being! Give this secret to him first, and you will discover that his outward life will be changed naturally and easily.

Accomplishing all this is very easy. How? Simply teach a believer to seek God within his own heart. Show the new Christian that he can set his mind on Jesus Christ and return to Him whenever he has wandered away.

Furthermore, show him he should do all and suffer all with a single eye to please his God. What a difference it will make. The new convert will be led to Jesus Christ; he will discover that the Lord Jesus is the source of all grace; and he will see that in *Him* is everything needed for life and godliness.

You, steward of men's souls, I urge you to lead these young ones in Christ in *this* very way. Why? Because this way *is* Jesus Christ. It is not I, but Christ Himself urging you by His own blood that was shed for these believers:

> Speak to the *heart* of Jerusalem.
>
> (Isaiah 40:2)

Preachers of His Word! Dispensers of His grace! Ministers of His life! *You* must establish His kingdom. In order to establish that kingdom, make Him *Ruler* over the *heart*.

I would emphasize again: The heart is the key. The heart alone can oppose His sovereignty. But counterwise, in gaining the heart, the Lord's sovereignty in the believers's life is confessed and highly honored.

> Give glory to the holiness of God, and He shall become your sanctification.
>
> (Isaiah 8:13)

Teach this simple experience, this prayer of the heart. Don't teach methods; don't teach some lofty way to pray. *Teach the prayer of God's Spirit,* not of man's invention.

Take note! You who teach believers to pray in elaborate forms and meaningless repetition! You actually *create* the major problem new Christians have. The children have been led astray by the best of fathers. The new believer has become *too* conscious of his style of prayer, too concerned with how to pray. Furthermore, he has been taught a language too refined and too lofty.

The simple way to God has been hidden.

Are you a Christian new to Christ? Go then, poor child, to your loving Father. Speak to *Him* honestly in your own words. No matter how crude and simple those words are, they are not crude and simple to Him!

It may be that your words will seem unclear and confused. It may be that at times you are so full of love and so awestruck at His presence that you do not know how to speak. That is all right! Your Father is *far* more pleased with *these* words—words which He sees pouring out from a heart that is full of love—than He could ever be by elaborate-sounding words that are dry and lifeless.

The simple, undisguised emotions of love express *infinitely more* to Him than the words of any language.

For some reason men try to love God by forms and rules. Can you not see it is by these very forms and rules that you have *lost* so much of that love?

How unnecessary it is to teach the art of loving!

The language of love is strange and unnatural to that man who does not love. Oh, but it is *perfectly* natural to the one who loves.

And how shall you love Him?

It is amazing and delightful to see that it is the simplest Christians who often progress farthest in an inner relationship with Jesus Christ! Why? Because the Spirit of God simply does not need our tapestry!

The simplest can know Him, and in the deepest way, with no help from rituals or forms or theological instruction! When it pleases Him, *He* turns factory workers into Prophets! No, He has not turned man away from the inner temple of prayer. The reverse! *He* has thrown wide *open* those gates so that all may come in!

> Whoever is simple,
> Let him turn in here.
> Whoever lacks understanding,
> Come.
> Eat of my food
> And drink the wine I have mixed.
>
> (Proverbs 9:4,5)

The Lord Jesus thanked the Father for having "hidden these things from the wise and intelligent and revealing them to babes." (Matthew 11:25)

24

The Ultimate Christian Attainment

We come now to the ultimate stage of Christian experience.

Divine Union.

This cannot be brought about merely by your own experience. Meditation will not bring divine union; neither will love, nor worship, nor your devotion, nor your sacrifice. Nor does it matter how much light the Lord gives you.

Eventually it will take an *act of God* to make union a reality.

In the Old Testament the Scripture says, "No man shall see God and live." (Exodus 33:20) If your prayer still contains your own life, that prayer cannot see God. *Your* life will *not* know the experience of union with *His* life.

All that is of your doing, *all* that comes from your life—even your most exalted prayer—must first be destroyed before union can come about.

All the prayers that proceed from your mind are merely *preparations* for bringing you to a passive state; any and all active contemplation on your part is also just preparation for bringing you to a passive state.

They are preparations. *They are not the end.* They are a *way* to the end.

The *end* is union with God!

The purpose of this book is not to show you prayer, or even experience, but to bring you to the final Christian state: union with God.

You will recall that John tells us in Revelation 8:1 that there was silence in heaven. This is a picture of the center of the inmost part of man. In that place all must be hushed to silence when the majesty of God appears.

The effort of the self must be stilled. But even more! The very existence of the self must be destroyed.

There is something in this universe which is the very opposite of God; it is the self. The activity of the self is the source of all the evil nature as well as all the evil deeds of man. On the other hand, the *loss* of the selfhood in the soul increases the purity of the soul! In fact, the soul's purity is increased in exact proportion to the loss of self!

As long as you employ your self nature in any way, some faults will also continue to exist in you. But after you depart from your selfhood, no faults can exist, and all is purity and innocence.

It was the entrance of the *self*, which came into the soul as a result of the fall, that established a difference between the soul and God.

How can two things so opposite as the soul and God ever be united? How can the purity of God and the impurity of man be made one? How can the simplicity (or singleness) of God and the multiplicity (endless fickleness) of man ever melt into one element?

Certainly much more is required than just the efforts that *you* can make.

What, then, is necessary for union to be achieved? A move on the part of Almighty God Himself. This *alone* can ever accomplish union.

For two things to become one, the two must have similar natures. For instance, the impurity of dirt cannot be united with the purity of gold. Fire has to be introduced to destroy the dross and leave the gold pure. This is why God sends a fire to the earth (it is called His Wisdom) to destroy all that is impure in you. Nothing can resist the power of that fire. It consumes *everything.* His Wisdom burns away all the impurities in a man for one purpose: *to leave him fit for divine union.*

There is impurity in you. More than you could ever conceive. And it is fatal to union with God. But your Lord burns to be one with you, so He *will* consume the dross. (Do not be surprised when this actually happens.)

What is the name of this impurity? Self. Self is the source of all defilement, and it prevents any alliance with Purity!

The rays of the sun may shine upon mire, but those rays will never be united with the mire.

But there is more than the self that prevents union.

This thing called *activity* is, in itself, opposed to union. Why? Because God is an infinite stillness. Your soul, if it is to be united with the Lord, must partake of His stillness.

Activity prevents assimilation.

It is for this reason we can never arrive at divine union except by putting the human will to rest. You can never become one with God, in experience, until you become as restful and pure as when you were first created.

God wishes to make your soul pure. He purifies it by His Wisdom just as a refiner purifies metal in the furnace. *Fire is the only thing which can purify gold.*

Again, the fire that consumes us—utterly—is His highest wisdom.

This fire gradually consumes all that is earthly; it takes out all foreign matter and separates these things from the gold.

The fire seems to know that the earthly mixture cannot be changed into gold. The fire must melt and dissolve this dross by force so that it can rid the gold of every alien particle. Over and over again, the gold must be cast into the furnace until it has lost every trace of pollution. Oh, how many times the gold is plunged back into the fire—far, far more times than seem necessary. Yet you can be sure the Forger sees impurities no one else can see. The gold must return to the fire again and again until positive proof has been established that it can be no further purified.

There comes a time, at last, when the goldsmith can find no more mixture that adulterates the gold. When the fire has perfected *purity*—or should I say *simplicity*—the fire no longer touches it. If the gold remained in the furnace for an eon, its spotlessness would not be improved upon nor its substance diminished!

Now the gold is fit for the most exquisite workmanship. In the future, if the gold should get dirty and seem to lose its beauty, it is nothing more than an accidental impurity which touches only the surface.

This dirt is of no hindrance to the use of the gold vessel. This foreign particle which attaches itself to the surface is a far cry from having corruption deep within the hidden nature of the gold.

Rare would be the man who would reject a pure, golden vessel because it had some external dirt on it, preferring some cheap metal only because its surface had been polished.

Please do not misunderstand me. I am not excusing sin in the life of a person in union with God. Such an idea never occurred to me. I am referring here only to natural defects; defects which God deliberately leaves even in His greatest saints, to keep them from pride and to keep them from the praise of men who judge only from outward appearance.

God allows defects to remain in the dearest of His saints so He can preserve that saint from corruption and "hide him in the secret of His presence." (Psalm 31:20)

Let us continue looking at the contrast between pure gold and impure gold.

Have you ever considered that a goldsmith would never mingle pure gold and impure gold togther? There is dross in the cheap gold; therefore, he will not allow it to be mixed with his costly, purified gold.

What will the goldsmith do, then? After all, he *wants* the two mingled together! What he must do is subject the impure gold to the fire. He will do this again and again until the inferior gold becomes as pure as the fine gold. Then, and only then, will the two be united, blended into one.

This very thought was in Paul's declaration:

> The fire will try every man's work, of what sort it is.
>
> (I Corinthians 3:13)

Then Paul added:

> If any man's work be burnt
> He shall suffer loss,
> But he himself shall be saved,
> Yet so as by fire.
>
> (I Corinthians 3:15)

Paul indicates that there are works so impure and so mixed that even though the Lord in His mercy accepts the man, that man must pass through the fire to be purged from *self*.

The same sense is found in Romans 3:20. Here God is said to examine and judge our righteousness. Romans declares that by the deeds of the law no man shall be justified; justification is by the righteousness of God, and justification is laid hold of by faith in Jesus Christ.

So you see, God's justice and God's wisdom must come like a pitiless and devouring fire. That fire destroys all that is earthly. The fire destroys the sensual, the carnal, and all self-activity.

All this *purging* is necessary *before the soul can be united to its God.*

You can be sure, dear reader, that you will *never* be motivated enough to allow this purging process to happen to you! Man, by his nature, is very reluctant to submit to such a transformation. All of us are greatly enamored with self and very fearful of its destruction. You can be sure you would never consent if it were not that *God* takes it upon Himself to act upon you. It is He who comes with power and authority.

God must take responsibility for bringing man into union with Himself.

But is this possible? Will God act upon man without man's consent? Is this a break with divine principles, an imposition of God upon the free will of man? After all, the idea of "man's free will" is that man can resist God's work in his life.

Well, let us return to that hour of your conversion. At that time you made an unreserved surrender of your being to God. Not only that, you surrendered yourself to *all* that God wills for you. It was at that very time that you gave your total consent to whatever God might wish to require of you.

Oh, it is true that when your Lord actually began burning, destroying, and purifying, you did not recognize that it was the hand of the Lord in your life. You certainly did not recognize the operation as something *good*. You had the very opposite impression!

Instead, you saw all that beautiful gold in you turning *black* in the fire rather than becoming bright as you had expected. You stood looking at the circumstances around you that were producing all that tragedy in your life. You thought that all the purity in your life was being lost.

If, at that moment, the Lord had come and asked you for your active consent, at best you would hardly have been able to give it. It is more likely that you would not have been able to give consent at all.

There is something you can do at times like those, however. You can remain firm in a passive consent, enduring as patiently as you can all that God has introduced into your life.

What am I saying?

It may be true that you cannot give to the Lord your active consent in such a dark and difficult hour, but neither are you able to put an obstruction in His way. You cannot say "yes." You cannot say "no.'

What can you do?

Pressed between these two points, you find you are capable of doing *nothing*. In such a situation you have given the Lord your *passive consent!* God is not usurping when He then assumes full power and total guidance!

Can you grasp the unfolding process?

You begin at conversion with *self-activity*. But gradually, although progressively, you move toward *passivity*. Along the way between those two points your soul is gradually purified of all those movements of the soul that are so distinguishable and full of so much variety.

In this process that lies between self-activity and passivity you begin to recognize those elements which separate you from God. (And the things I have mentioned in this chapter *are* those elements which are between you and your Center.) Then, by giving your passive consent to the purging fire of God, He takes you, degree by degree into a more and more passive state.

Your capacity for becoming passive is gradually increased. Your capacity to be passive before God and under the crushing of the cross (to say neither an active "yes" nor an active "no" to His dealings) is enlarged in a secret, hidden manner.

You are now passing through the first stage of being drawn into the depths of God. He is *conforming* you to His purity.

But there are two stages in God's drawing you. The second stage is *uniformity* with God.

We have seen that there is a progress in the first stage of being conformed to God. There is also a progress in the second stage.

Self-effort gradually decreases. Eventually, it ceases altogether. When self-effort ceases, your will is passive before God.

You have come to uniformity.

This is beyond a passive state. Or at least it is the ultimate end of the passive state. It is at this point you begin to yield yourself up to the impulses of the divine Spirit *until you are totally absorbed* with Him. You are in total concert with His will in all things—at all times.

This is union. Divine union. The self is ended. The human will is totally passive and responds to every movement of God's will.

I need not warn you, *this* is a process that, indeed, takes a long time.

Was activity and effort involved in order to arrive at such depths in Christ? Yes. Activity is the *gate*. However, we should not tarry at the gate. In fact, your aim, your tendency, must always be toward one point: ultimate perfection.

Please know that all the "helps" and "crutches" must be laid aside along the way or the ultimate goal cannot be attained. Yes, the self nature is not only laid aside but so are all the "helps" which I introduced to you at the beginning of this book. Those are elemental crutches to aid you in your *beginning* and in the *process*. But all things must ultimately be laid aside as we reach the final depths in Christ.

These helps were very necessary at the entrance to this road, but later they are actually detrimental. Even so, some Christians will still stubbornly cling to these crutches.

This is what made Paul declare:

> Forgetting those things which are behind
> and reaching forth to those which are
> before, I press toward the mark
> for the prize of the high calling
> of God *in* Christ Jesus.
> (Philippians 3:8)

Here is a traveler. He has launched out on a long journey. He comes to the first inn, and there he remains forever. His reason? He has been told that many travelers have come this way and have stayed *at this very inn*; even the master of the house once dwelt here.

Surely our traveler has taken leave of his senses to remain at the first inn for no more reason than this.

Oh soul! All that is wished for you is that you press toward the end. Take the shortest road, the easiest road. It has now been mapped out for you. Only remember this: Do not stop at the first stage.

Follow the counsel of Paul: Allow yourself to be led by the Spirit of God. (Romans 8:14) That Spirit will unerringly conduct you to the end purpose for which your soul was created. That end purpose is the enjoyment of God.

Stop for a moment and just see the reasonableness of the path before you.

First, we all have to admit that God is the Supreme Good. Surely, then, the ultimate blessedness is union with Him.

And every saint has glory *in* Him, does he not? Yet the glory in each of us is so different. Why? The glory differs according to the degree of that Christian's union with God.

As we have seen, the soul cannot attain this union by effort or by mere activity or by its own power. This is because God alone communicates Himself to the soul of man—and He communicates Himself in proportion to the soul's capacity to remain passive. A great, noble, and extensive passive capacity aids the Lord in pouring Himself into the soul.

Next, you can only be united to God in simplicity and passivity. Simple, in that God is all and passive in that the human will is in accord with the divine will in all things.

This union is beauty itself. Therefore, it follows that the way which leads into passivity—and from there on to Christ—could not possibly be anything but good. This way is the one most free from danger, and it is the best way.

But is there danger in knowing union with God? Some say, "Yes," and discourage even the idea of it. But would your Lord have made this experience, this perfect walk, this necessary way, if it had been dangerous? No!

Such a state is available to all, and the way there can be travelled by all.

All of the Lord's children have been called to the

enjoyment of God—an enjoyment that can be known both in *this* life as well as in the life to come. Our state in that day will be one of eternal happiness in union with God. *Our call in this life is the same.*

As we near the end of this book, a few thoughts are in order.

I have been speaking to you of an enjoyment of God, not of the gifts of God. Gifts do not constitute the ultimate beatitude. *Gifts cannot satisfy your soul* or your spirit. Your spirit is so noble and so great that the most exalted gifts God has to give cannot bring happiness to the spirit. . .not unless the Giver also gives Himself.

Dear reader, the whole desire of the Divine Being can be described in one sentence: God wishes to give Himself utterly to every creature that names His name. And He will do this, giving Himself to each of us according to our individual capacity.

But alas! Man is a remarkable creature! How reluctant he is to allow himself to be drawn into God! How fearful, how remarkably fearful he is to prepare for divine union.

One last word.

Someone is almost certain to tell you that it is not right that you put yourself into a state of union with God.

I totally agree.

But I add this word: No one *can* put himself into union with God. It would not be possible, no matter how great the effort. The soul's union with God is something God alone does. There is therefore no purpose in speaking out against those who seem to be trying to unite themselves with God; such a union (God with self) is not even possible.

You may also find someone saying to you, "Some people will hear of this and claim to have attained this state when actually they have not." Oh, dear reader, such a state cannot be imitated any more than a hungry man, on the verge of starving to death, could convince you he was full.

A wish, a word, a sigh, a sign, *something* will inevitably escape him and thereby betray the fact that he is far from being satisfied.

Since one cannot attain union with God by his own labor, we do not pretend to introduce anyone to it. All one can do is point out the way that eventually leads there. Oh yes, and one other thing—one can beseech the seeeking soul not to stop somewhere along the way.

(Dear reader, don't settle somewhere on the road or become attached to the external practices that first got you started. All these, such as praying the Scripture and beholding the Lord, must be left behind the moment the signal is given to you.)

One who is experienced in helping others knows he can't take another Christian into this relationship with God. All he can do is point to the water of life and lend his aid to the seeker. This much, of course, he can do and must do. It would be cruel to show a spring to a thirsty man and then bind him in such a way that he could not reach the stream. Some speak of divine union but never allow the seeker freedom from his shackles. This does happen, and the poor saint eventually dies of thirst.

Then let us agree on this: There is divine union, and there is a way to it. The way has a beginning, a progress, and a point of arrival. Furthermore, the closer you come to the consummation, the more you put aside the things that helped you get started.

Of course, there is also a middle, for you cannot go from a beginning to an end without there being an intermediate space. But if the end is good and holy and necessary, and if the entrance is also good, you can be sure the journey between those two points is also good!

> Oh the blindness of the greater part of mankind which prides itself on science and wisdom! How true it is, Oh my God, *that You have hidden these wondrous things* from the wise and prudent, and have revealed them unto babes!
>
> J.G.

25

From Prison

During Jeanne Guyon's first imprisonment in the city of St. Antoine, France, some letters sent to her from the outside reached her. She was allowed to answer at least a portion of these inquiries. A few of the letters which Jeanne Guyon wrote in response have survived.

One letter she penned was in answer to a woman who had recently read this very book and had written asking a number of practical questions. Jeanne Guyon's reply is preserved for us. It is fitting to close this book with excerpts from that remarkable letter.

It is a great pleasure to hear of the manifestations of God's mercy toward you and to see the progress of your soul in spiritual experience. May God bring to completion the works He has begun within you. I am sure He will if you continue to be faithful.

Oh, the unspeakable happiness of belonging to Jesus Christ! Belonging to Jesus Christ is the true balm which sweetens all those pains and sorrows which are so inseparable from this earthly life.

Let me venture a few practical remarks.

When you are reading, stop now and then for a few

moments; give yourself to waiting on God and to prayer in silence. Especially do this when you have read a passage that touched you. Let the reading have an appropriate effect. Respond to that sense *within you that came as you read the passage. Respond to His touch.*

Reading in this way will edify you and nourish your soul.

Yes, your inward parts—your soul and your spirit—need nourishment just as your body does. Unless your soul is nourished with something that strengthens it, the spiritual state of your soul will simply wither and decay.

As to your body, I recommend that you not *engage in inflicting mortification on it yourself. Your feeble health does not allow for it. If you had a strong body and if you allowed yourself to be ruled by your appetite, I would probably advise you differently.*

But there is a kind of mortification which I do recommend to you very earnestly. Mortify *whatever there is that remains of your corrupt* affections *and* desires*; mortify your own will; mortify your taste, your disposition, the things you are naturally inclined to; mortify your habits.*

For instance, learn to suffer with patience. God will send frequent and probably great suffering into your life. This is His doing; He has chosen it; accept it.

Learn to suffer all that happens to you—even confusion*—but learn to do so out of only one motive: love for God. Accept everything, whether it be ill treatment, neglect, or whatever else may come your way. To sum up what I am saying: You can mortify your being by bearing at all times, in a serene way,* *everything that thwarts your natural life. Put to death the disagreeable feelings which rise up inside of you when unpleasant things enter your life. In so doing, place yourself in union with the sufferings of Christ.*

Bitter remedies, true. But by taking them you will honor the cross.

You most especially honor the work of the cross in you if you die utterly *to everything that is showy and attracting about you. But this death does not take place outwardly. Mortification and death take place in your inward experience.*

Learn, then, the lesson of becoming a little one, of becoming nothing. A man who fasts—leaving off all those things his appetite improperly craves—does a good thing. But the Christian who is fasting from his own desires and his own will, and who feeds upon God's will alone, does far better. This is what Paul calls the circumcision of the heart.

Lastly, it appears to me that you are not yet *sufficiently advanced in inward experience to practice silent prayer for a long, uninterrupted period of time. I think it would be better for you to combine spoken prayer with silent prayer. Release such expressions as these to your Lord:*

"Oh my God, let me be wholly Yours."

"Let me love You purely for Yourself, for You are infinitely lovely."

"Oh my God, be my all! Let everything *else be as nothing to me."*

Offer up these and other such words; offer them up from your heart. But I think such expressions should be separated from each other by short intervals of silence.

It is in this *way you will gradually form the important habit of silent prayer.*

Take the Lord's Supper as often as you can. Jesus Christ, who is in *that ordinance,* is *the bread of life. He nourishes and enlivens our souls.*

I shall remember you as I worship before Him.

May He set up His kingdom in your heart and reign and rule in you.

Jeanne Guyon
from prison
St. Antoine, France

Epilogue

A HISTORY OF THIS BOOK

This book has one of the most incredible histories of any book ever written.

A Method of Prayer made its first appearance in France in about 1685. Immediately, God used it as an instrument to stir believers all over France. Opposition was also immediate. You are holding in your hand a book that has been publicly burned! Nonetheless, its popularity has always equalled its opposition. For instance, a group of Roman Catholic priests came into the town of Dijon, France, where the Lord was touching many lives through this book. The priests, opposed to both the book and the work the Lord was doing in Dijon, went door to door and gathered up a total of 300 copies and burned them! Three hundred copies of one book is a remarkable number to be found in one town during the 1700s.

One Frenchman took 1500 copies and passed them out all over his community. As a result, the whole town was profoundly affected.

Of all Jeanne Guyon's writings, she is best remembered for her autobiography and for this little work, but it was *this* work, now entitled *Experiencing the Depths of Jesus Christ*, which provoked the political and religious system of her day to launch out against her. Along with a copy of the book she wrote entitled *Song of Songs*, this book was placed in the hands of Louis XIV as evidence that she should be arrested. Later, before a religious tribunal, these writings were cited as the main evidence against her. On the basis of this book she was denounced as a heretic and imprisoned, eventually, in the infamous Bastille.

Such was the history of this book during the lifetime of Jeanne Guyon. But that was no more than a starter. The men and the movements that Jeanne Guyon has influenced would themselves fill volumes. I will cite a few.

Shortly after her death, it appears, the early Quakers began using this book and, probably more than any other single piece of literature, it affected their whole movement. In fact, though the Quaker movement was over a hundred years old before it came upon this book, Guyon probably influenced the Quakers spiritually as much as did their founder George Fox.

Next to be influenced by this book was Zinzendorf and the Moravians.

Still later, an earnest young man named John Wesley read the book (along with Jeanne Guyon's other works) and was profoundly moved by it. Its influence on his life partly explains his deep piety and spiritual depth.

The "Holiness" movement of the late 1800s with its emphasis on sanctification must trace its genesis through Wesley to this book and its author. (The charismatic movement which began in the early 1900s, with its awesome power and incredible shallowness, signalled the end of the forward thrust of the holiness movement and an emphasis on spiritual depth among the many off-shoots of Wesleyism. In fact, the idea of tongues and empowerment pre-empted virtually all emphasis on *the deeper Christian life* in that movement and many others!

Next, Jesse Penn-Lewis, a dominant spiritual figure at the beginning of this century, was greatly influenced by the works of Jeanne Guyon.

Many other groups and movements have been influenced by the writings of Jeanne Guyon, but one of the greatest influences this book has ever had was during the 1920s in China. At that time this book reached a young man destined by God to be one of the best known of His servants in this century. The book fell into the hands of young Watchman Nee. Along with the *Autobiography* of Jeanne Guyon, it constituted one of the major influences on his life; and as a result, the book became an indirect influence on the lives of many of his co-workers.

There were other men and other movements affected by the writings of Jeanne Guyon, but I believe you see the point. The extensive effect of this book becomes even more amazing when you realize that it has been — from the very first edition — almost impossible to understand! Even in the original French version, the book is vague and complicated with a vocabulary at once so exacting and yet so obscure that reading it has always been a study in frustration. The English translation did nothing to help.

Despite all this, you still hold in your hand a work that has influenced the lives of more famous Christians than perhaps any other piece of literature penned in the last 300 years.

Eventually, as you might expect, the book went out of print; for over 50 years it has been virtually forgotten. During this time, as far as I know, the only available edition in circulation was a very, very poor one put out in mimeographed form!

Should you think that I exaggerate in describing the difficulty of understanding Jeanne Guyon's writings, you might try this passage:

> Do you ask why this course is pursued? The whole object of the way thus far has been to cause the soul to pass from multiplicity to the distinct sensible without multiplicity; from the distinct sensible to the distinct insensible; then to the sensible indistinct, which is a general delight much less attractive than the other. It is vigorous in the beginning, and introduces the soul into the perceived, which is a purer and less exquisite pleasure than the first; from the perceived, into faith sustained and working by love; passing into this way from the sensible to the spiritual, and from the spiritual to naked faith, which, causing us to be dead to all spiritual experience makes us die to ourselves and pass into God, that we may live henceforth from the life of God only.*

Now that you have read this very typical paragraph out of her writings, I hope you will not think too ill of us for having changed the wording of some of the more vague passages. If we had not done so, there would have been little point in re-issuing the book.

**Union with God*

Most of the truly helpful Christian literature penned on the deeper Christian experience was written after 1500 and before 1800. (Little of lasting weight, it seems, has been written in either this century or the last.)

Unfortunately, some of the best Christian literature on the deeper Christian experience is imprisoned in the incomprehensible language of other centuries. Among the best of all this literature — and the most difficult to read — are the works of Jeanne Guyon.

In chapters one through four, Jeanne Guyon shares with you a unique way of "praying the Scripture." You will find it an awesome experience. In recent years an adaptation of her method appeared, but you will see from reading this book that she never intended anyone to stop there. She had *far* greater oceans for you to discover and never intended for you to remain in these shallows.

Should God so see fit, it is our hope that you will have a chance to read, in modern English, other works from the pen of this feminine vessel.* Let me explain why.

THE PRESENT STATUS OF SPIRITUAL EXPERIENCE IN THE CHURCH

Since the end of the first century, no century has excelled in spiritual depth. In fact, most centuries

*Christian Books Publishing Company has now published five of her books, *Union With God, Guyon's Spiritual Letters, Song of Songs, Genesis, Spiritual Torrents* and has re-issued her biography, written by T.C. Upham.

since then have been very, very shallow indeed with only a handful of gloriously shining lights — usually no more than a few dozen men and women — to illumine the darkness.

This era — the one you and I live in — has proven to be, unquestionably, the most Bible-centered age since the days of the Pharisees; it also rivals their age for being one of the least in emphasizing spiritual depth! (And men today get just as disturbed as men of that former age did, when someone points out that fact!)

Nor is that the only record our age has set. We are setting a whole raft of records. For instance, until today the 1500s have generally held the trophy for being the most financially corrupt age in church history. That was the day you could — for cash — have your sins erased right out of God's ledgers. We don't do that, but with our mass mailing, business reply envelopes, four color brochures, foundations, professional fund raising campaigns, "living by faith," tax exempt status, and sermons on stewardship, by the time he is 35 years old, many ministers of the gospel have become some of the best promoters and fund raisers around.

The same can be said for intellectualism. The 1700s have usually been considered the high water mark of intellectualism in the Christian faith, but today more men walk the earth with doctorates in theology than in *any* other age. Unsatisfied with the spiritual depth this intellectual climate has produced, these men cry out that the solution is more, better, and higher Christian education. This is an age of endless reams of books and papers on endless varieties of subjects, an age that produces men who deliver mind-boggling lectures on the *doctrine* of prayer and yet know little of its deeper experience. This age has, generally, *never* known Christ in a deep way. Sophisticated, disdainful, sterile and passionless, we have wrenched from the hand of the 1700s the tropy for the most intellectual age in church history.

The era between 1100 and 1400 has generally been considered the darkest and most corrupt in church history, an age when the papacy went to the highest bidder and the church was the most powerful political and financial force on the earth.

But we live in a day when churches look like storybook castles. Servants of God today, looking back upon the first century worker's idea of owning *nothing* throughout his whole life, might view such an ideology as cultish. They are quite unlike their fathers, the early Christians, who were the natural enemies of their community, who fought for the *privilege* of living their whole lives owning nothing but the clothes on their backs, and who gloried in dying as might a pauper.

Those of us who are serving the Lord "full time" in this age should prepare ourselves for being remembered, as a whole, as being the wealthiest, most commercial, sophisticated, worldly-minded, materialistic and comfortable men in the whole history of religion.

There is one more trophy which this age — above any other — will win (that is, unless a radical change takes place very soon). In every era of church history there have been recorded the names of a few devout men and women whose hallmark was awesome spiritual depth and utter devotional abandonment. There were such men even during the bleakest days the dark ages ever witnessed. In every age there have *always* been at least a few men who knew Him in the depths. Will our age slip by with no such testimony? From a purely historical viewpoint, we *must* be categorized as the most universally shallow believers ever to cross the pages of church history.

It is my studied judgment that some future generation will deem this to be the darkest century, in spiritual depth and spiritual experience, in church history — that is, *unless* something very radical happens along...soon.

More corrupt than the dark days before Luther; more impotently intellectual than during the heyday of Calvinism; more financially perverted than the days that caused John the Baptist to explode; more intoxicated with the drive for spiritual power than any age, yet exercising that outward power with less internal transformation than anyone since King Saul; enamored with the gifts, yet hardly knowing the Giver, our age has produced the most commercial, materialistic, fad-oriented people ever to claim His name.

Is this assessment a little too harsh? I would respond to you by pointing to one last trophy this age may win: We seem to be more totally blind to the deprivation of our spiritual depth than all other centuries lumped together.

It is true we have built more buildings and founded more religious organizations than all the past eras combined. It is true that today's Christianity has won more men to Christ than all other ages combined, but it is also just as true that those converts have set new records for the short length of time they have followed the Lord with abandoned devotion.

If past church history is any guide, we can optimistically look for some sort of a turnaround. Spiritual depth is due for a return! I can think of no one better qualified to gain our attention, melt our hearts and introduce us to some of the depths of Christ than the lady who penned this little book.

May God see fit to so bless us in an age of such spiritual shallowness.

THE FUTURE OF THIS BOOK

There seems to be a revival of interest in the life of Jeanne Guyon. If so, I trust that one day the Roman Catholics will take a new look at one of their most distinguished daughters. Rome has often put its servants to death and later turned around and sainted them. Catholicism has never produced, by *their* standards, a woman more qualified to be canonized than Jeanne Guyon.

While we are on the subject of the Roman Catholic Church, I would like to make this observation. It is amazing that Roman Catholicism, with so much of its traditions, rituals and teachings rooted in paganism, has consistently produced *more* devout followers of Christ than we Protestants! The deepest Christians in church history have consistently *not* been Protestant! The Catholics rank second, the Protestants rank third in giving church history its deepest Christians and in illustrating the deeper Christian life and a passionate, torrential love for Jesus Christ.

Who ranks first? If you look closely, you will find sprinkled throughout all the centuries of church history *little bands* of Christians — neither Catholic nor

Protestant — who have borne the mark of this abandonment.*

This book will probably find a warm reception in all three groups. In fact, it runs the danger of being so well received that it will not get the disciplined attention it requires.

There is a vast Christian audience that literally devours "devotional" literature as fast as it can be taken off the printing presses. I have a notion many Christians will find here merely one more devotional book to read, to contemplate, to apply for a few days, and then to lay aside.

Then there are those who will turn the contents of this book into a series of sermons on prayer.

This revolutionary treasure deserves a better fate.

There are some readers, though, who will recognize the unique character of this book and the spiritual depth of its author. These are Christians who will take the path pointed to by this book and drink deeply of a great *internal* adventure. For such a reader, there is waiting the most marvelous, precious, and probably the most unexpected discovery he will ever know: the inexhaustible riches found in encountering Jesus Christ.

If you happen to fall into this category, I would like to express a concern. I have a notion the Lord would

---

*Some of the groups, who have been neither Protestant nor Catholic and who have appeared throughout the centuries as pure and faithful followers of Jesus Christ, are the Cathars, the Priscillianists, the Paulicans, the Bogomils, the Waldensians and Albigenses, the Lollards, the Unitas Fratrum, the Moravians and the Brethren. You may wish to read *The Torch of the Testimony*, which tells the story of these people.

very much like to get past this business of isolated Christians getting isolatedly blessed and "deep in Christ." It is my hope that very soon we Christians will get past sitting at home like spiritual misers hoarding up deep experiences with Christ...and, instead, move toward a more corporate adventure of the deeper Christian life.

That brings us to another category of Christians, and it is for you, primarily, that this book was issued. It is you, above all others, who I hope will get hold of this book and not let go until all its contents have become reality.

To whom am I speaking?

To those who have a heart to launch out on the great but terribly perilous adventure of the restoration of church life.

Allow me to explain.

THE ISSUE OF THIS AGE

Jeanne Guyon once made the observation that in every era *God* raises a spiritual issue. During Paul's life it was "works and faith." Every age since then has also had its controversy; and in every age since Constantine, our God has set about restoring those precious experiences of the early church that had been lost. In her own age God used Jeanne Guyon to raise the issue of the *indwelling* Christ. That is, that the Lord is within you — working from the inside out — that you can know Him and experience Him by living in that inner chamber where He makes His home. (It would still make a good issue today!) She raised the issue of the *interior* Christ.

But God did not stop raising issues with the 17th Century. He raises yet other issues; He is a restoring God.

Is there a spiritual issue in our age?

Well, if there is not, there should be! If men and women today, by the thousands, began experiencing the depths of Jesus Christ in a real and transforming way, there would be simply no place for their experience to fit into the present-day rites of Christianity, be they Protestant or Catholic forms. Neither movement is presently structured to contain a mass of devoted people who walk in spiritual depths. Or, to put it another way, both movements *are* structured toward other emphases; it is, by its nature, a structure that hinders the torrents of unleashed love meant to be poured out on God. The very element, the very soul, the very composition and structure of present day Protestantism and Catholicism frustrate a deep encounter with the living God!

When you visualize a people who love Christ with a passion, who are utterly abandoned to Him, a people who know Him well and know nothing else on earth but Him, does a Sunday morning church service come to your mind? A people such as I have just described simply cannot fit — not for long anyway — into the structured mold of mainstream Christianity.

A revival of an experience of Christ in the depths will naturally issue into a longing for this indefinable thing sometimes called "church life."

What is "church life?" I do not know how to give a definition, but it is the church glorious, stunning and all-consuming; the church jealous, devouring your whole life; the church magnetic, claiming every moment of your being; the church living and *free*; the church winged in flight. Not a place, but a people — living in the heavenlies, constantly consumed with *Him* and *blind* to all else. The church as she once was, ought to be, can be, *will* be! A bride — passionate, wooing and madly in love with her Lord and her Love. A people who know and experience Him!

Consider this, dear reader: Jesus Christ loves you. He saved you. You love Him. That is one reason you are reading this book: to know Him better. You, an individual, wish to *know* Him. But God *never* intended for you to pursue Him *solely* as an *individual*.

Please remember that half the New Testament is written to *churches* not individuals! (Laying aside the four biographies of the Lord, nearly *all* the New Testament is addressed to churches. Churches: vibrant, free, loose. Churches that met in homes, whose people shared each other's lives and loved one another — and their Lord — indescribably.) Those churches were incredible — not so much in being free of problems, or in being morally perfect, but in their corporate, daily pursuit and experience of Jesus Christ, in the sheer joy of knowing Him together, daily, constantly.

May this become the issue of *someone's* age! Yes, the issue of the restoration of the *experience* of that beautiful thing called the church.

You and I have no alternative if we plumb the infinite depths of Jesus Christ; eventually we will be driven to the issue of the life of the church. God's ultimate desire is not that you be rich and happy, or that you have a nice devotional life, or a thousand other things you might think. Reread the record. The passion, the centrality of the Scripture is Christ and the church. You and I cannot know Christ as we should without also knowing the living experience of the church.

You cannot have salvation without a living Christ. You cannot have the full ends of the deeper Christian life without a living experience of Christ *and* a living walk inside the experience of church life.

God simply set up His grand design with Christ and the church as the *center*. He made it the very nature of things. You can fight it if you choose, but you cannot beat it; God made Christ and the church *central*. The fact is in the very bloodstream of the universe. You can try some other approach, but it won't work. You are moving *against* God's designs. Christ and the church are the sum total of God's schemes. The universe flows in that direction; any other way is upstream.

You need Christ — not in your mind, but in a consuming encounter. You need the church — not as a stone building, but the very outliving of your whole day, your whole life.

So, dear reader, this book goes forth for all of God's people, but this time it goes forth mostly for those who wish to experience the depths this book speaks of in the context of the life of the church. It will be only the Christian who places himself in the atmosphere of church life who will know the full depths of Christ. It seems the Lord made things so that His *fullness* is known only there.

The Old Testament told all about Christ, but when men of old read the Old Testament, they did not see Him there. God is like that. He keeps His highest revelation slightly veiled. Why? So men will not trample it underfoot.

But then one day Christ came! All at once God lifted the veil. Men could turn to the Old Testament and so easily see Christ all through it! But at the same time God lifted the veil on the old, He did something else! He placed a veil over the new. While Christ lived on the earth, men who heard Him could not quite get the full meaning of His words. Christ was veiled to all except His handful of disciples (and even His disciples did not fully understand Him until their Lord came *into* them).

Since the days of Constantine (325 A.D.), a great deal of God's original purpose has been lost. Since the Reformation, since Luther, God has been restoring those things, but He continues the principle of veiling His *present* work on the earth. While He lifts the veil on the last thing He restored, He turns and veils His newest activitity. He does this to keep the things dear to Him from being cheapened.

We are told, for instance, that 80 percent of all evangelical and fundamental teachings today came from the Plymouth Brethren movement of the early 1800s. That seems to be an established historical fact. But you could never have convinced theologians in the early 1800s of that!

It was not until the mid-1800s that the mainstream of Christianity began to read the writings of the Brethren and, finally, realized the wealth that was there. Forthwith ministers began preparing sermons based on what they read of Brethren writings. The Sunday morning congregations were very impressed. But structure could not handle *everything* the Brethren had said. What they taught had to be watered down a bit to fit.

The problem was easily solved; men simply left out

the main point. (Now you know why God veiled His work among the Brethren for a whole generation.)

But why did the Lord ever allow the work of the Brethren to come into public view anyway? Why did He ever allow their wonderful insight and experience to become common and diluted? It seems that when the Brethren's message became good sermon material for Sunday morning sermons, their major contribution to church history began to end.

Why? Because He had moved on. God had moved on, leaving the brethren as one of his *past* works. He had moved on to do a work of recovery *somewhere else,* a deeper work, and a work hidden from full view.

The Lord has moved on through several Christian movements since then. What is hidden in one generation is preached as Sunday sermons during the next generation. The Lord then moves on, giving to a new work the original insight of the first and *adding* to that revelation...giving them whole new realms to discover, to experience, and to restore.

Today ministers all over the earth are proclaiming things revealed to obscure little groups of the last generation.

(Today's ministers are also bringing breathtaking messages on things they know absolutely nothing about and have never experienced. Essentially, they are repeating what they have read in books. And the people sitting in the pews listening are very impressed. The cutting edge, of course, has been left out.)

Do not mourn or weep. It is all right. Somewhere on the earth today our God is moving onto higher revelation and to new plateaus of restoration!

Now, what has all that to do with this book?

Just this: For nearly 300 years the contents of this book were kept from the general reading public. Why? I think probably because it contains a few of the highest insights and deepest revelations of the secrets of *experiencing* Christ that have ever been put down on paper. But for 300 years — because of the obscure language in which it was written — God allowed this book to walk through history partially hidden from view.

That is quite a compliment to the author and to the book! It is almost as though God has had to wait nearly 300 years before opening it to general view because there has been nothing deeper and richer to succeed it.

The book now goes forth. As a book, it has few — if any — peers. But somewhere God has moved on! His revelation of experiencing His Son has once more been broadened; new realms have opened. The book still has no equal, but the experience recorded here is not where God has rested. Somewhere out there our Lord is poised to move farther in and higher up.

HOW TO USE THIS BOOK

What is the best way to make use of this book? It is by giving it a great deal of your time. One other word. In years to come I would highly recommend that you return to this book again and again. Its message enlarges the more you mature in Christ. The message of this book will arrest you at 20; it will stir you at 30; it will break you at 40 and still be calling you deeper into Christ in the years beyond.

Return again and again.

When this book first fell into my hands, it was in the form of a very clumsy, mimeographed edition. Whoever prepared that simple edition had added a preface. I still recall the essence of the opening words. I will close this epilogue with those words. They went something like this:

> That this little book has fallen into your hands is an indication that God desires to do a special work in your heart.

THE STORY OF
MADAME GUYON'S LIFE, by T.C. Upham 9.95

If you enjoy reading Jeanne Guyon's writings, you will wish to read the story of her life. Through the centuries a multitude of Christians have held it to be the most outstanding life story of any Christian woman in church history. Truly one of Christendom's best known and most frequently read biographies.

Her well-known autobiography ends at age 40, whereas she became an internationally known figure and spiritual influence in Europe after that time. The best of her life story is not included in her remarkable autobiography. T.C. Upham's history of her life, on the other hand, recounts her fame in the Court of Louis XIV, her clash with Bossuet, her trial, the international storm created by Fenelon's clash with Bossuet over her teachings, her imprisonment in the dungeon of Vincennes, her four years as a prisoner in the infamous Bastille.

One of the half dozen truly great Christian biographies.

EXPERIENCING THE DEPTHS
OF JESUS CHRIST 4.95

Guyon's first and best-known book. One of the most influential pieces of Christian literature ever penned on the deeper Christian life. Among the multitudes of people who have read this book and urged others to read it are: John Wesley, Adoniram Judson, Watchman Nee, Jesse Penn-Lewis, Zinzendorf, and the Quakers. A timeless piece of literature that has been on the "must read" list of Christians for 300 years.

UNION WITH GOD 4.95

Written as a companion book to EXPERIENCING THE DEPTHS OF JESUS CHRIST, and includes 22 of her poems.

SONG OF SONGS 5.95
GENESIS 5.95

Jeanne Guyon wrote a commentary on the Bible; here are two of those books. SONG OF SONGS has been popular through the centuries and has greatly influenced several other well-known commentaries on the Song of Songs.

THE SPIRITUAL LETTERS OF MADAME GUYON 6.95

Here is Jeanne Guyon at her very best. There is a Christ-centeredness to her counsel that is rarely, if ever, seen in Christian literature. Among her writings, next to EXPERIENCING THE DEPTHS OF JESUS CHRIST, we would recommend this book.

SPIRITUAL TORRENTS 9.95

The last book ever written by Madame Guyon. This is a *limited* edition that will not be reprinted and, therefore, will probably not be available beyond 1984.

THREE BOOKS BY GENE EDWARDS:

THE DIVINE ROMANCE cloth 12.95

The most powerful, arresting book we have ever published. With a might and beauty that sweeps from eternity to eternity, here is, truly, the greatest love story ever told. If you have any interest at all in the deeper Christian life, then, by all means, read this book. Rarely has the depth and mystery of Christ been put so simply, yet so profoundly.

A TALE OF THREE KINGS 4.95

A book beloved around the world. A dramatically told tale of Saul, David and Absalom, on the subject of brokenness. A book used in the healing of the lives of many Christians who have been devastated by church splits and by injuries suffered at the hands of other Christians.

OUR MISSION 9.95

A group of Christian young men in their early twenties met together for a weekend retreat to hear Gene Edwards speak. Unknown to them, they were about to pass through a catastrophic split. These messages were delivered to prepare those young men spiritually for the inevitable disaster facing them. Edwards presents the standard of the first century believers and how those believers walked when passing through similar crises. A remarkable statement on how a Christian is to conduct himself in times of strife, division and crisis. A book every Christian, every minister, every worker will need at one time or another in his life.

CLASSICS ON THE DEEPER CHRISTIAN LIFE:

PRACTICING HIS PRESENCE 4.95

The monumental seventeenth century classic by Brother Lawrence, now in modern English. (One of the most read and recommended Christian books of the last 300 years)

The twentieth century missionary, Frank Laubach, while living in the Philippines, sought to put into practice Brother Lawrence's words. Included in this edition are excerpts from Frank Laubach's diary.

THE SPIRITUAL GUIDE 5.95

At the time Jeanne Guyon was teaching in the royal court of Louis XIV (in France), a man named Michael Molinos was leading a spiritual revival among the clergy and laymen of Rome! He actually lived in the Vatican, his influence reaching to all Italy and beyond. The great, the near great, the unknown sought him out for spiritual counsel. He was the spiritual director of many of the illuminaries of the seventeenth century. He wrote THE SPIRITUAL GUIDE to meet the need of a growing hunger for spiritual direction. The book was, for a time, probably the most popular book in Europe, but was later banned and condemned to be burned. The author was convicted and sentenced to a dungeon after one of the most sensational trials in European history.

Here, in modern English, is that remarkable book.

CHURCH HISTORY:

These two books bring to bear a whole new perspective on church life.

THE EARLY CHURCH 4.95

This book tells, in a "you are there" approach, what it was like to be a Christian in the first century church, recounting the events from Pentecost to Antioch. By Gene Edwards.

THE TORCH OF THE TESTIMONY. 6.95

John W. Kennedy tells the little known, almost forgotten, story of evangelical Christians during the dark ages.

The prices listed here are for 1984 only. Write for a complete catalog and updated prices; also let us know if you would like to be notified of future releases.

(Christian Books also sponsors a conference on the deeper Christian life each summer in New England.)

Order the above books from your favorite Christian bookstore or from Christian Books. (No C.O.D. or billing. Please enclose payment in U.S. funds.)

CHRISTIAN BOOKS PUBLISHING HOUSE
P.O. Box 959
Augusta, Maine 04330

If you are just getting acquainted with books on the deeper Christian life, we would like to suggest what may be the best approach to reading books on this subject. There is not a great deal of literature available in this area of the Christian walk, so you will wish to make the most of what is available.

We recommend that you begin your reading with THE DIVINE ROMANCE. Follow with EXPERIENCING THE DEPTHS OF JESUS CHRIST and PRACTICING HIS PRESENCE. THE DIVINE ROMANCE will stir and give insight and prepare you for the practical and spiritual help found in the other two books.

Two other books which compliment EXPERIENCING THE DEPTHS OF JESUS CHRIST are UNION WITH GOD and THE SPIRITUAL GUIDE.

You will also find real profit in reading THE SPIRITUAL LETTERS of Jenne Guyon and THE SPIRITUAL LETTERS of Fenelon. Many of the questions and problems of your daily walk with Christ and your relationship with others are dealt with in these two books.

For insight into brokenness and to see just what the heart of a man of God should be, the beautiful A TALE OF THREE KINGS is a book you will want to read again and again. If you would like to know more about the ways and purposes of the cross, suffering and transformation (which must come into the life of all Christians), then you will want to read THE INWARD JOURNEY.

DIVINE LIFE might be looked upon as a technical explanation of the human spirit and its difference from the human soul, but having read this book, you will be pleased to know more about the spiritual process going on inside you. This book is a great help to Christians in their quest to get a handle on their spirit.

THE EARLY CHURCH, Volume I, the story of the body of Christ from Pentecost to Antioch, will give you insight into what "church life" meant in the first century.

THE TORCH OF THE TESTIMONY tells the story of the church and church life as it survived during the dark ages and beyond.

PUBLISHER'S REQUEST

We plan to publish a new biography of the life of Jeanne Guyon and are now in the process of gathering all material still available. Do you know of any new research that has been done on her life during this century, that is, since Upham wrote a biography at the end of the 1800's? If so, we would appreciate knowing about it.

We would also appreciate knowing of any living scholars who are authorities on her life.